D0853860

FOWLER HIGH SCHOOL LIBRARY

ADOPTION CONTROVERSIES

$ 15.95

B + T

12-15-93

ADOPTION CONTROVERSIES

KAREN LIPTAK

THE CHANGING FAMILY

FRANKLIN WATTS

NEW YORK ▲ CHICAGO ▲ LONDON ▲ TORONTO ▲ SYDNEY

Library of Congress Cataloging-in-Publication Data

Liptak, Karen.
Adoption controversies / Karen Liptak.
p.   cm. — (The Changing family)
Includes bibliographical references (p.   ) and index.
Examines the various forms
of adoption, as well as foster
care and surrogate mothering,
focusing on the prospects
and disadvantages faced by
both child and parent.
ISBN 0-531-13032-0
1. Adoption—United States. I. Title. II. Series: Changing
family (New York, N.Y.)
HV875.55.L56   1993
362.7'34'0973—dc20   93-19810   CIP

Copyright © 1993 by Karen Liptak
All rights reserved
Printed in the United States of America
6 5 4 3 2 1

CONTENTS

ADOPTION CONTROVERSIES

THE HUMAN SIDE OF ADOPTION

"When you're infertile, you go through tremendous highs and lows. There's always this possibility, and then you get your period and you're normally depressed anyway and it's a bottomless pit. The thing that always happens is that you're led on by doctors every step of the way, and my doctor never said to me 'I have good news for you.' And the first time our social worker came to visit us she knew that we would get a child from this agency and so she said, 'I have good news for you. You're going to be parents.' And when she said that, I broke down and cried, because nobody had ever said that to us before, and it was like this dream that was going to come true."
—Adoptive mother of two children

"I want to keep my baby, but it seems so cruel to want to take care of her when I can't even take care of myself. I know the pain is terrible, but it's better this way."
—Birthmother who is giving her child up for adoption

"I've lived in six foster homes in the last six years. My dream is to have a family that can love me. I'd rather have that than anything at Christmas."

—Foster child, aged 8

"It's not that I want to disrupt her life, but I want to get on with my own. That's why I've been hunting for the last two years."

—Adoptee who has been searching for her birthmother

The voices of adoption are heard everywhere you go, from coast to coast, because adoption touches the lives of millions of people in this country. There are 6 million adoptees which means that there are 12 million birthparents and perhaps 12 million adoptive parents. When you add grandparents, you may have 24 million birth grandparents and 24 million adoptive grandparents who all play a tremendous role in the adoption. That could bring the total to 78 million people who are intimately affected by adoption. Perhaps you know or are a birthparent yourself. Perhaps you are an adoptee, or are living in a foster home, or may even be engaged in a search to find the birthparents who had to give you up many years ago.

To people raised by their birthparents, adoption may seem like a foreign concept; they never think about it beyond, perhaps, knowing that a classmate or neighbor is adopted and therefore is "different" from them. Yet the possibility of having to decide about consenting to adoption (the term for allowing one's baby to be adopted) can suddenly strike home for any teenager faced with the dilemma of an unintended pregnancy.

Statistics show that unplanned pregnancies among teenagers have reached what some experts call "epidemic proportions." According to a recent study at the National Center for Health Statistics, teenage motherhood is at its highest level in fifteen years.[1] Despite major campaigns to educate teenagers about sex and its risks of disease and unwanted pregnancy, about 1 million teenage girls in the United States—including one out of every ten aged fifteen to nineteen—become pregnant every year. Some experts give today's fourteen-year-old girls a 40 percent chance of getting pregnant by the time they are twenty.[2]

Even if the birthparents are very much in love, they may decide that they aren't ready to take on the financial, emotional, and time commitments of being full-time parents, let alone husband and wife.

When an unmarried girl becomes pregnant, she generally faces three major options: abortion, parenting a child, or consenting to adoption. Placing a child for adoption is also called "relinquishing a child." Whichever option is chosen, each has its own consequences and its own controversies.

Adoption is currently the least popular of the choices available to teenagers and other pregnant females. According to the Guttmacher Institute, a private research group focusing on reproductive health and family planning, about half of the estimated annual 3 million unwanted pregnancies in the United States end in abortion, making it the most popular choice. Of the 1.5 million babies born each year following an unwanted pregnancy, only 2 percent are placed for adoption.[3]

African-American and Hispanic unwed mothers have always had very low relinquishment rates because their extended family system was often able to absorb an unplanned child into the immediate family, or the home of a close relative like an aunt or a sister. But, before 1973 almost 20 percent of unwed *white* mothers gave up their babies. That percentage has dropped dramatically in the past twenty years, resulting in a drastic reduction of babies in the adoption pool. One reason for this downswing is the availability of legal abortion since 1973. Another reason is that single motherhood no longer carries the stigma it once did, when raising a child born out of wedlock was unthinkable. With the divorce rate so high, many biological children are being raised in one-parent homes, so being a single parent is much more acceptable than ever before. Single moms are heroines on many television shows, and in many communities, today's teens face intense family and peer pressure to keep their unplanned child even if it will be raised by the grandparents. Pregnant teens are often made to feel that only terrible people give a baby away and that it is in the child's best interest for them to bring him or her up, regardless of their circumstances at the time.

"The child's best interest" is a phrase heard very often among adoption experts. To adoptive parents, it is in the child's best interest to be placed with them. To many birthparents, it is in the child's best interest to stay with them. However, there is one thing most people can agree on: There are no easy answers where the adoption triad—birthmother (and her partner), adoptive parent(s), and adoptee—is concerned. Adoption is an emotional subject filled with many dilemmas and debates. And, as we explore its many facets, we touch upon our most basic values and our feelings about what constitutes a family and what best serves a child's developing identity.

Many in the adoption field believe that society would best be served if more unplanned children were placed for adoption. This is certainly the opinion of thousands of potential adoptive parents, many of whom long for a child but find that they cannot, generally for medical reasons, have a biological son or daughter. They are ready and willing to give a child all the financial and emotional support they can provide. All they need is a birthmother willing to relinquish her child to them. On the other hand, many others believe that society would best be served if family preservation were given more support, so that any mother or father who wants to keep a child can do so.

But, before we explore the controversies that adoption brings up, let us consider the other options available for a pregnant teenager. As you will discover, none of them are perfect solutions. Instead, each underscores the fact that there are no easy answers to a teenager's unplanned pregnancy. When a girl discovers that she is pregnant, much time and energy must be spent making a decision that will affect many people: the mother-to-be herself, the birthfather, the birth grandparents, the unborn child, and the prospective adoptive parents as well.

One final word. There is no hidden message here, no bone to pick, nor subtle point to make. The author is not a member of any adoption triad. But, like many of you, I know many people who are themselves members of adoption triads. I have also spoken to many professionals in the adoption community, (or as its critics say, "the adoption industry"). And quite frankly, there are many, many times when it is very easy to see the validity of every point of view in any given controversy.

What I have tried to do is present an up-to-date, unbiased introduction to the world of adoption controversies. For some, this will serve as a research tool. For others, who are now part of a triad, or who may be considering the possibility of becoming part of one, I hope this book provides them with some help in a world in which loving families are both precious and difficult to create.

2

TODAY'S OPTIONS FOR UNWED PREGNANT TEENAGERS

▲ ABORTION

It may surprise you to learn that abortion is one of this country's most common surgical procedures.[1] Contrary to what many think, abortion is not a relatively new concept. It was regularly used in eighteenth-century colonial America, but a movement to limit abortion began in the late 1800s. By the 1950s, every state had outlawed abortion, except in extreme cases. Then came the 1960s and abortions increased again, representative of the liberal attitude of the times, with its strong support for the individual's right to choose. In 1973, the Supreme Court's famous *Roe* v. *Wade* decision legalized abortion. *Roe* v. *Wade* declared that the right to choose an abortion is derived from the right to personal privacy.

Ever since the *Roe* v. *Wade* decision, anti-abortionists in the United States have been trying to eliminate or curtail abortion rights. In 1992, the Supreme Court heard arguments on a Pennsylvania law to restrict abortion in that state. The result was a "mixed decision" by the Court that upheld these major points of Pennsylvania law: women seeking abortions must be told about alternatives and fetal

14

development; women must wait at least twenty-four hours after getting information; doctors must keep records subject to public disclosure on each abortion; unmarried girls under age eighteen must have their parents' consent. The ruling is seen by many as a step toward overturning *Roe* v. *Wade* and turning the right to abortion into a privilege. Deborah Leavy, the executive director of the American Civil Liberties Union of Philadelphia, said that the twenty-four hour waiting period in the Pennsylvania law would be especially hard on poor women in rural areas who find it difficult to get to a doctor's office twice. Abortion rights advocates claim that the ruling also hurts teenagers, because they will have to get a court order if they cannot tell their parents that they are pregnant and want an abortion. "To find an abortion provider is a big step. Then to go to court—it's going to be very difficult," says Ms. Leavy.[2]

The decision allows states to limit abortions, even though the majority of Americans believe that having one is a right of privacy that should be protected. To Senator George J. Mitchell of Maine, abortion is a constitutional right and "we do not allow states to restrict other constitutional rights."

Currently, abortion rights supporters are trying to get a bill passed that will have the right to an abortion established by *Roe* v. *Wade* written into federal law. The object of the bill is to prevent the disappearance of abortion rights, which a weakened *Roe* seems to be leading to.

As mentioned earlier, most pregnant teenagers choose to have an abortion. According to the *Journal of the American Medical Association*, a well-performed abortion is five to ten times safer than childbirth, and teenagers have fewer complications from abortions than do older women. Those who decide not to terminate their pregnancies often base their decision on religious grounds, even though approximately one-third of the women who have abortions are Catholic, and abortions are against church doctrine. Others veto an abortion because it is too difficult to obtain, especially in rural areas, or it is against their personal code of ethics or their cultural beliefs.

According to Patti Caldwell, education director with Southern Arizona Planned Parenthood, when a young woman comes to them to find out if she is pregnant, she receives a pregnancy test; it takes less than ten minutes. A medical assistant gives her the results of the test. If the young woman is pleased with her pregnancy, the medical assistant proceeds to tell her about the kinds of education, referrals, and prenatal care she needs. If the mother-to-be is anything other than thrilled about her condition, the medical assistant lets her know that free pregnancy counseling is available. This counseling is made possible through public and private grants to every woman, regardless of her financial situation. The girl leaves with the referral sheet that contains prenatal care, adoption information, and abortion information. On the top of the sheet is a statement reminding the girl that regardless of her decision there can be challenges and difficulties ahead and that counseling remains available.

"The medical assistant isn't programmed for any particular option," reports Ms. Caldwell. "Their role is to make sure the person knows she has options, to get her the referral sheet, and let her know there is a pregnancy counselor if she wants to talk."

Ms. Caldwell finds that younger teenagers are harder to reach. Sometimes, after the family of a younger teen recovers from the shock of an unplanned pregnancy, they are there with support, whereas a seventeen- or eighteen-year-old's parents may be annoyed with the young person's behavior or feel that if she is old enough to get into this predicament, she is old enough to get out of it as well.

Counseling at Planned Parenthood can continue for up to one year after an abortion, or after delivery if a woman chooses to have her child. The counselor's job is to help the mother-to-be examine all of her options to be sure that she is thinking realistically; to help her sort through her

16

own personal strengths and weaknesses, and her family support, so that she can reach a decision she personally is comfortable with; and to support her in the decision, regardless of what the counselor feels. Ms. Caldwell says that frequently parents call, wanting their daughter to see a counselor and terminate the pregnancy. "There's no way she's ready to be a parent," the birthmother's parent may say. But the counselor's client is the mother-to-be, and if she wants to have that baby, then it becomes the counselor's job to be her advocate, even if it means helping her to explain how she feels to her own parents.

According to Ms. Caldwell, the growing trend among young women to carry pregnancy to term is primarily due to the climate in our country regarding abortion. She believes that schools don't give enough information about pregnancy options, and, as a result, young people are ignorant about them. Lack of access and finances further limit a young woman's choices. "There are very few agencies in the country that have funds that help subsidize abortions for women who don't have money," says Ms. Caldwell. Government assistance is available in only thirteen states.

An abortion during a woman's first trimester at Southern Arizona Planned Parenthood costs approximately $275, which includes pregnancy testing, screenings and treatments, sonograms, and everything else that is needed. For a young person or poor adult woman, that expense is prohibitive. And the lack of a local abortion provider for women who live outside cities necessitates travel, which a woman may be unable to do because of her work schedule or her inability to afford transportation.

But no matter what the choice is or what happens in the future concerning abortion, the abortion debate is particularly charged for adoptees and adoptive parents. Some see a woman's decision to abort as depriving potential adoptees of life and depriving potential adoptive parents of children.

If abortion is not a choice, then a pregnant teenager will elect to have her child. This decision may be made out of conviction or by default. It is not unusual for teenagers to postpone telling their parents about their condition until physical changes force them to admit the obvious. By then, even those who might have chosen to have an abortion may find that option no longer possible.

Most teenage girls who do give birth raise the baby at home, either by themselves or with a close relative. In some cases, the teenager chooses to raise the baby, and then finds out that she was being unrealistic, in which case the grandparents may adopt the baby and raise it as their own or the child may be relinquished for adoption later on.

Unfortunately, in many cases, when a young woman chooses to parent her baby, she is paving the way to a lifetime of poverty, since she may have to drop out of school to support the child. According to statistics, most of the nearly 600,000 teen mothers who keep their babies are poor and unmarried. Twenty years ago, there were far fewer unwed mothers because their partners often married them, whether out of love, guilt, duty, or fear of parental disapproval. Today, such "shotgun weddings" are far less common.

And even when a teen couple facing an unplanned pregnancy marries out of love, their future is on shaky ground. Often the young man and woman grow apart and break up through no fault of their own; they simply become less compatible with their spouse as a natural consequence of becoming more in tune with themselves. According to many adoption experts, in the majority of current cases, the teen father abandons the mother and child, leaving her to face alone what may be the most emotionally painful episode in their lives.

The new mother who is left on her own and unable to finish school will find that her lack of education can lead to reduced job opportunities and even a life of welfare in a single-parent home that may very well mimic her own upbringing. There are other statistics to consider: A girl who has a baby at fifteen or sixteen is likely to have at least one other child before she is twenty. Given the stresses on a teenage mother's family, and the inability of many teenagers to properly care for their children, many of their babies wind up being abused or in foster care.[3]

The trend to keep an unplanned baby is especially prevalent among younger girls. Adoption experts say that those who relinquish for adoption are generally older teens who are better able to separate themselves from their child and make the difficult but realistic decision about what is in that child's best interest. Patti Caldwell explains that girls of twelve to fourteen or so tend to be very concrete in their thinking. Because they are not yet ready to think in the abstract, they can't remove themselves from the situation and examine what is best for them and for the potential life growing inside them. As Ms. Caldwell explains, "It's a developmental issue . . . you can't teach that thought process."

According to Lexanne Downey from Catholic Social Services of Tucson, Arizona, bringing up a child is "kind of a status symbol." She says that young girls who have goals in life are more likely to choose adoption than those who have "nothing to look forward to. To women in that situation," she says, "a baby looks pretty good."

Yet the possibility of a young mother's life suffering from a decision to keep her baby is very real unless she has a strong, supportive family or she gets outside help, generally in the form of social services. Researchers claim that the best way to help unwed teenage mothers is to enable them to get a high school diploma, rather than drop out to support a baby. Studies have shown that teen mothers who graduate from high school have a better than even chance of getting good jobs, meeting their babies' financial needs, and reaching the same income level as their classmates. As a result, new programs have been started to encourage teen mothers who keep their babies to stay in school.

In the past decade, over 300 schools in 46 states have started parenting and child-care programs for teen mothers. Most of the programs are financed by a combination of public and private funds. However, there are still far too few programs to handle the 800,000 children of teen mothers who need child care each year.

Some teen-parenting programs, like Rindge and Latin's, in Cambridge, Massachusetts, are housed within regular high schools. Other programs around the nation provide teen mothers with separate schools that have day-care centers. Administrators of these programs say that they can offer more comprehensive services, and some teen mothers prefer being with students in the same circumstances.

New Futures School in Albuquerque, New Mexico, is considered a model of this type of school. Before giving birth, the students receive prenatal health care, counseling sessions, and childbirth classes. Later, they can take child-development classes while their children stay in on-site nurseries; there are four nurseries, each for a different age range. The students can even breast-feed during class. Schools of this type serve the mothers as well as the babies.[4]

Depending on where a girl lives, she may also find programs that offer her a place to stay while she is pregnant, and after she gives birth, so that she can stay in school. There are also a variety of programs throughout the country that provide counseling in offices, schools, or in the girl's own home. Patty Short, who runs one such program in Tucson, Arizona, usually spends about one hour each week with each of her clients. Most of the discussion revolves around advice on being a parent. Ms. Short also tries to bolster the self-image of the woman.

Her role varies from giving out information on health care programs to being a sympathetic listener and sharing a mother's sorrow when the baby's father chooses to leave her.

Another valuable program in Tucson is run by the Center for Adolescent Parents. Begun in 1987, it offers job training, parenting skills, and tutoring classes for high school equivalency tests. Potential participants usually learn about this and other such programs through school counselors, mental health centers, family service agencies, health departments, family planning clinics, and crisis pregnancy centers.

▲ THE ADOPTION OPTION

Just the mention of adoption as an option is controversial. Many people in the adoption community believe that adoption is not given enough consideration as a viable option for birthmothers. They claim that marriage, single parenting, and abortion are emphasized, but it is considered wrong for a woman to carry the baby to term only to give it up.[5]

Meanwhile, people like Joe Soll, C.S.W.—who is an adoptee, a therapist, and founder of the Council for Equal Rights in Adoption, a worldwide adoption search and support group—say that birthmothers are being coerced into adoption by both agencies and lawyers. They believe that, in reality, the best thing for mother and child is to preserve families so that women are not "separated from their babies except in the most extreme circumstances."

Although adoption is the option chosen by only the minority of birthmothers, the exact number of children released for adoption is difficult to pin down. As critics of the adoption system often say, the government may have a state-by-state "hog report" but it doesn't know accurately how many children are adopted. In the past it was known that certain doctors would enter maternity patients in the name of the adopting mother, who had been negotiated with before.[6]

Where adoption is the option of choice, the birthmother's usual motivation is love for the unborn child, and the feeling that this is the best choice for the child. These birthmothers realize that at the time of their pregnancy they are not able to give their offspring the time or material stability a child needs. The birthmothers may still be in school, just starting out in demanding careers, or not emotionally or financially stable enough to be responsible parents.

While therapist Joe Soll acknowledges that there will always be children who will need adoption, he is adamant about the dangers of taking a child away from its mother simply to serve another person's needs, since he believes that there is a psychic shock at the moment of separation that affects both mother and child. According to Mr. Soll, there is "a billion dollars a year on processing fees to get children and so there is a vested interest in many quarters in doing that separation."

On the other hand, as one adoptive mother strongly believes, "In our society, if a young woman keeps an unplanned pregnancy, people will normally say 'at least she didn't give it up for adoption.' Very few, if anyone, support women who are brave enough to give a child they have born a better life. It [adoption] should be given a whole different set of values than the ones in society. It takes a whole lot of bravery and courage to make that kind of decision."

Indeed, while adoption is often chosen with the noblest of motives, there is no getting around the fact that it causes great pain and sorrow for the birthmother. It is not an easy decision to relinquish a child, even if you know that your son or daughter is going into a fine and loving home.

Advice about adoption is not hard to come by, but

it can be confusing, and it takes some searching to find nonjudgmental advice. Making the decision to relinquish a child for adoption is just a first step. Next comes a decision about what type of adoption to choose. Today, birthparents have many more choices than in the past about the kinds of adoption available.

This book is about adoption controversies. As you will quickly learn, there is no hard and fast way to best handle an adoption. Each birthparent and adoptive parent has to face several dilemmas. Should the adoption be open or closed? Should it be through an agency, independent facilitator, or perhaps a mixture of both? Should the birthparents insist on adoptive parents who have similar backgrounds to theirs? Should a transracial adoption be considered? What about single parents adopting your child? Physically challenged parents? An older couple? And what if a child you plan to relinquish is born with a handicap? What are his or her chances of being adopted? What is foster care all about? How does being adopted or being fostered affect a growing child? What is the likelihood of an adoptee and his or her birthparents being reunited? What rights do birthparents have? What rights does the child have? Basically, all the questions boil down to a basic one: What is in the best interest of everyone—the birthparents, the adoptee, and the adoptive parents?

As you will discover, the story of adoption is changing as the complexion of adoptive families changes. In the not too distant past, infertile couples (those unable to have children of their own) were the only people who could adopt. Usually, they tried to have biological children for many years, then went through great emotional pain as they came to terms with their infertility and chose to create their family through adoption.

Today, adoptive parents are also couples with birth children, as well as single parents, homosexuals, physically challenged adults, and others. Agencies continue to place babies, as well as "special needs" children—infants who are not white, older children, those with physical and/or emotional handicaps, as well as sibling groups.

Today, the majority of prospective adoptive parents want healthy white infants. Less in demand are the "special needs" or "waiting" children mentioned above. Although we are most familiar with adoptions through agencies, you will find that there are other avenues for adoption matches to be made. Independent placements take place entirely outside an agency's domain. There are also identified or designated adoptions, in which a match may be made outside an agency, and then the adoptive parent(s) and/or the birthparent(s) go to an agency for counseling and other services.

How the Adoption Process Works ▲ Since there are no uniform laws of adoption, each state has its own laws as well as requirements. Whether a young woman places her baby through an adoption agency or through a lawyer, it is important that she be informed of all the rights she has under the law in her state. A pregnant young woman may first consider adoption during counseling sessions at a crisis pregnancy center, family planning clinic, health department, or mental health center. The counselor she talks to should provide her with the information about rights and regulations in her state. Otherwise, she can get this information by contacting her state's department of public welfare or the National Adoption Information Clearinghouse (NAIC) at 301-231-6512. NAIC, established by Congress, provides many free factsheets on adoption issues, as well as listings of adoption agencies, crisis pregnancy centers, counseling agencies, and other adoption-related services.

A woman who has an adoption plan needs to know that she has a right as a birthparent to see and care for the baby as much as she wishes while in the hospital. Legally speaking, until she signs the adoption papers, her rights are the same as those of any other mother. On a more psychological level, the current trend by adoption specialists is to encourage birthmothers to care for and name their newborns before relinquishing them. The specialists claim that this allows the birthmothers to begin to grieve and makes the experience real to them.[7]

If the birthparents can't make a decision in the hospital, they have the option of putting the child in foster care for a brief period of time while they consider what to do. Lexanne Downey of Catholic Social Services urges birthmothers to have contingency plans, just in case they planned on adoption but change their mind at the last minute. Otherwise, they're not prepared to parent a child, and that adds to the stress of the situation. However, if they decide to keep the baby, this is not necessarily irrevocable. Adoption will still be available for them later on.

In an independent adoption, the baby is generally surrendered by the birthmother directly to the adoptive parents, or to a lawyer representing them. If the adoption is through an agency, the baby is usually surrendered to a representative of that agency who in turn places the child in a foster home, sometimes called a "cradle home," which provides a short-term placement for the child until the necessary release papers are completed. Foster parents, like adoptive parents, must be approved by the state. Another possibility in agency adoptions is for the potential parents to become "legal risk" foster parents. These are foster parents who take in a child with the intent to adopt once the child becomes available. In that case, the baby may be placed directly with the potential adoptive parents, and remain with them until the adoption is legalized.

In Arizona, surrender, or release, papers are signed by the birthmother seventy-two hours after the child is born. Requirements for birthmother surrender differ from state to state. Requirements for birthfather surrender also differ from state to state. In Arizona, the birthfather is required to sign the consent. If he does not appear, a sufficient search for him must be conducted, and if he is still not found, his rights must be severed through the court (see the chapter Rights of Birthfathers). Otherwise, as soon as the relinquishment papers have been signed, the baby can be placed in a permanent adoptive home.

Once the child is with the adoptive parents, there is still a time period—each state sets its own—before the adoptive parents can petition the court to finalize the adoption. Under Arizona law, for instance, finalization does not take place until at least six months after a baby is placed with a family. Before finalization, a post-placement supervision report must be made to the court by the adoption agency. When an adoption is finalized, it is binding and irrevocable. The birthmother or her partner cannot suddenly decide to take the child back. They no longer have any legal rights to, or responsibility for, the child.

Each state has a public or state agency that oversees children in their care in that state, and this includes foster care and adoption. Such agencies may be called the Bureau of Family and Children's Services, the Division of Social Services, or the Department of Public Welfare. Public agencies usually have local branches throughout the state.

States also license private adoption agencies, both for-profit and nonprofit. Some of these agencies may have certain specialties, such as placing older children or children from foreign countries.

Independent placement, while legal in most states, has different laws governing it. Each state department of social services should be able to provide information about what is legal in that state. Finally, if an independent placement is being considered across state lines, the interstate compact, which establishes procedures for the transfer of children from one state to another, must be applied.

Home Studies ▲ The differences between agency and independent adoptions will be discussed in a later chapter. However, in either kind of adoption, the potential adoptive parent(s) will need to have a "home study" in order to be certified by the state. During a home study, a social worker will try to determine if the potential new parents will make good parents. In interviews, the potential adoptive parents will have to answer many questions about their decision to adopt, the strength of their marriage, their finances and employment, their attitudes toward bringing up children in general, and toward raising children who were born to someone else in particular. Potential adoptive parents will be asked what kind of child they are open to, and what problems they would find difficult to handle (for example, a child born as a result of a rape or a child who was the victim of child abuse). If so, the next question is what type of child would be best to place with them.

Home studies have evolved to now include group counseling sessions at which adoptive parents learn parenting techniques and get information about what adoption entails. In a sense, this is a self-eliminating device. As a result of these meetings, some people may discover that adoption is not right for them. The group meetings also help adoptive parents form networks with others wishing to adopt. Most home studies are done through agencies, but they can also be conducted by independent social workers. In the case of independent adoptions, the home study is often done through the court system.

Besides having to go through a home study, many adoption agencies and private lawyers require the potential parent(s) to fill out a lengthy application form. This form might be shown to the birthmother or birthparents, depending on how "open" the adoption is. Open versus closed adoptions will be covered in the next chapter.

After the adoptive parents have petitioned the court or made their formal request to gain legal custody of a child, and the adoption is finalized, the legal records collected for the adoption petition are sealed in the state's bureau of vital statistics. The baby's original birth certificate, with the names of the baby's birthmother and birthfather on it, is one of the records that is sealed away. It can only be seen again by order of the court. In its place, a new birth certificate is issued; this one lists the adoptive parents as those the child is born to. (Agency records containing medical and personal history may go to the adoptive family or may be kept by the agency.)

Today there are sealed-record laws in forty-seven states; the exceptions are Kansas, which is totally open, and Alabama and Alaska, which make records available to adoptees over eighteen. Other states require the consent of a birthparent, the child, and one or both adoptive parents before documents may be unsealed. Even then, a judge may rule against unsealing documents.

In California, which is considered a lenient state, a law passed several years ago allows an adoptee to obtain, at age twenty-one, the name and address of his or her birthparents if permission is on file from the birthparents to grant this disclosure. Birthparents are allowed to change their minds and later grant or revoke their permission by sending a notarized letter by registered mail to the agency. The Los Angeles County Department of Adoptions asks that birthparents let them know when they have health problems that might affect the child.

In both agency and independent adoptions, the birthmother's expenses may be paid for by the adoptive parents. However, having one's medical bills paid is not a basis for making an adoption plan. And even if financial costs are covered, nobody will say that choosing adoption is an easy option. Few birthmothers can surrender a child without feeling much emotional pain, even if they truly believe that the decision is in the child's best interest. Many birthfathers are similarly affected.

3 OPEN VERSUS CLOSED ADOPTIONS

"My own children came to me when they were two and three years old—they were in foster care because of abuse and neglect—and I adopted them two years later. I have some information about their parents; mostly the bad stuff. And the kids say stuff like 'I guess my mom couldn't take care of me because I was bad.' I can't say, 'I'll ask your mom,' or 'Your mom said this,' or 'Let's write your mom and ask.' I can't even tell them if their mom is dead or alive. And what I've learned, being in this business and having adopted children of my own, is that secrets are simply not healthy. What is really wonderful about the openness is that everyone wins with this. I really believe that."

—Michael Baker, clinical psychologist
and adoptive parent

"I'm liberal in lots of ways, but I can't see open adoption working for me. What happens when my kids are teenagers? What if

they suddenly decide to go live with their biological mother because she's more cool than
we are? No. I think that it's best the way we
have it. When they hit eighteen, they're free to
look for their mother. That's as far as I'll go."
—Susan S., adoptive mother of two toddlers

One of today's biggest adoption controversies is over open versus closed, or confidential, adoptions, with open adoptions at the moment appearing to be the wave of the future. In closed, or "traditional," adoptions the birthparents and the adoptive parents have no contact and little if any information about them is exchanged. After the adoption is finalized, the child's records are sealed by the court. In the past, the birthparents were advised to do the "unselfish thing" and put the child behind them so that all concerned could get on with their lives. The adoptee might then grow up thinking that his or her adoptive parents were the only ones he or she had ever had. Sometimes the adoption became a family secret, with everyone who knew about it sworn to secrecy. In other cases, the child was told about being adopted, but was not given any encouragement to search for the birthparents about whom the adoptive parents had scanty, if any, information.

This attitude is changing, with a movement toward adoptions that are to some degree open so that birthparents and adoptive parents exchange information and establish contact with each other. The contact can take a variety of forms depending on what the parties involved feel most comfortable with. It could consist of no more than letters and phone calls, perhaps with the adoption agency acting as liaison. At Catholic Social Services in Tucson, the birthmother or birthparents record an audio tape that is available for the adoptive parents to hear when they are ready, and which they can allow their child to hear at their discretion.

In some cases, openness may result in the birthparent becoming part of the child's extended family, whether for the first few years or throughout the adoptee's life. The birthparent might visit the child and share holidays with the adoptive family or she may have no more contact than a yearly picture of the child sent by the adoptive parents. In any case, a system is set up so that the birthparent and adoptive parents know how to get in touch with each other should the need arise.

For birthparents, there would seem to be many benefits to open adoption. They get to know how their child is doing. They don't have to wonder if the child is healthy or happy or even alive. Adoptive parents benefit by knowing about their child's origins. When questions come up, as they inevitably do for children who know they are adopted, they can provide answers.

Yet open adoption has not won over everyone. Even some very liberal adoptive parents feel uncomfortable with the concept. They say that forcing a child to deal with two sets of parents is confusing and detracts from a child's sense of permanency. They also worry that at any moment the birthparents may decide they want the child again and will find a way to reclaim it. Equally distressing is the thought that the child may someday choose to return to the birthparents, despite all that the adoptive parents have done. This, claim adoptive parents, is particularly threatening during an adoptee's adolescent years, a stage of life when individuals question intensely who they are and where they belong.

Another argument against open adoption is that the confidentiality is of supreme importance to some birthparents who would rather put their past behind them and forget they ever went through an unplanned pregnancy. This is especially true for birthparents who carried to term a child conceived in a rape.

Susan S., an adoptive mother, did not meet the birthmother of her first child, but consented to meet the birthmother of her second child. In retrospect she questions her decision. "I think when you don't meet the birthmother there are no expectations about what the child is like. I can't even remember her (the birthmother), but I do remember her fragility. I wish I hadn't met her. I'd rather think of her in totally superlative terms."

Yet supporters of open adoption maintain that no matter what the truth reveals, it is better than secrecy. On medical grounds, we now realize that it is important to know our genetic inheritance; such knowledge can help us anticipate future health problems, both for ourselves and for our children.

For many adoptees there is also a strong psychological reason to support open adoptions. Many experts in the field maintain that children have a great hunger for roots, for understanding where they came from and what their birthparents were like. Without such knowledge, say the experts, there remains a hole in the adoptees' lives, an incompleteness. Others, however, believe that there is danger in revealing "skeletons" in the family closet.

Today, more and more birthparents want open adoption, and a growing number of adoption agencies will only consider potential adoptive parents who accept at least some degree of openness. Whether this is out of compassion, or in response to competition among "baby brokers," is a matter of opinion. As one birthmother who gave up her child for adoption in 1967 noted not too long ago, "In the sixties, the catchword was, 'We'll protect you, we'll give you anonymity.' That was the sales pitch. The sales pitch of the eighties is openness. Promise the birthmother openness, and you'll get her baby."[1]

Janet Dawes, of the Arizona Children's Home (ACH), feels that communication within the adoption circle benefits everyone: birthparent, child, and adoptive parents. Otherwise, the birthparent is always there, "a ghost or shadow effect on your life." It is the adoptive parents who are often the most resistent to open adoption, with fears that some call irrational and others feel are justified.

Some say that open adoption is still too new a practice to determine if it really works better than traditional adoptions. However, Joe Soll, of the Council for Equal Rights in Adoption, says that records are open in almost every country in the free world outside the United States. This country's approach to adoption appears to be in the minority.

He notes that in 1991 the United Nations and UNICEF had a very important treaty ratified by eighty-one countries. Known as the Treaty of the International Rights of the Child, it states that all children born in this world have a right to know where they come from, to meet their family, to know their heritage. It was not ratified by the United States.

So far, in many cases in this country, open adoption seems to be working well. Those adoptive parents who opt for an open adoption feel that it can only benefit children to know that more people than their adoptive parents love them. Yet open adoption is not for everyone. As clinical social worker Priscilla Misner says, "Certainly, there are some birthparents who can't handle that [open adoption] very well and wouldn't be respectful of how critical it is for their children to feel that they belong in their adoptive families, and that those parents are their real parents, their psychological parents."

The ACH encourages birthparents and adoptive parents to meet before placement and decide how open they want to be with each other. Frequently, the two sides don't share last names, and the agency acts as a liaison, allowing them to communicate after the adoption. But, in some cases, the adoptive parents as well as the birthparents attend the birth. The adoptive mother may even be the birthmother's labor coach.

Before a home study is begun, potential adoptive parents at the ACH are invited to an initial orientation meeting. Whenever possible, at least one adoptive mother and birthmother attend this meeting with "their child." The prospective adoptive parents then hear both sides of the story of an open adoption that is working.

"I had the choice of whether or not to have contact with her before I had my child. When I was seven months pregnant I met her. My mother was there with me, and we talked about what we wanted the adoption to be. At first I picked to have pictures and contact in letters. Wanting to see him, that came after I delivered. I thought about it and I wrote in a letter asking if it was okay if she would allow me to see my child. We decided four times a year would be good for now until he gets old enough. If he decides he still wants to have contact when he's older that's fine. If not . . . it might hurt . . . but when I see Jesse happy that makes me happy because I know that he's happy where he's at. I personally think that open is the best way to go."

—Kathy, Jesse's birthmother

"I had adopted two girls, one when she was two years old and one when she was six years old. All I knew about those girls' moms was their names, so when I had a chance to adopt and it was an open adoption, it felt that it was that much more whole. And, to be honest, I felt relieved when we met and all she [Kathy] wanted was pictures and letters. And then, when I was at Jesse's birth and shared with Kathy that labor and that love . . . we were connected far deeper than letters and pictures. But, still, when Kathy wrote, asking to see Jesse, I couldn't help but get nervous. It had been perfect until then and I felt like, let's not rock the boat. But then Kathy and I got together again . . . and I asked her a lot of questions to find out why she wanted to keep the contact. And when I saw her I felt she loved him and I know that Jesse also loves her, and has a place for Kathy and a place for me. I love it. I love that Kathy can just pick up the phone and call me. . . . I would also add that having Jesse in an open adoption has been very healing for my other daughters, who are now ten and fourteen. They do believe that they were bad . . . and when they see how Kathy loves Jesse and Jesse couldn't possibly be bad they feel better about themselves. The experience of Jesse coming into our lives has just been a miracle."

—Teresa, Jesse's adoptive mother

Nancy, an adoptive mother of three children, also chose an open adoption. This came after her first adoption, which was closed because Nancy felt that she could not handle an open adoption then. But when her son began asking questions about his birth, she realized how inadequate she was to answer them. She began to feel that how you handle your adoption has a real impact on how you parent your child, and she chose to make her second and third adoptions open ones. Once she and her husband got to know the birthmothers and their situations, she says that "even had something fallen through it would have made it a lot easier because that would have meant it would have worked out for them."

Nancy felt that her second adoption was very special because the birthmother invited her friends to gather for a celebration at which everyone prayed for the situation. Although on paper the adoption was simply a legal transfer of parental rights, the ceremony put it on a much different level for Nancy. As she explained, the event "gave us permission to parent the child because we really felt like we had been gifted with a child and not as if we were taking someone else's child."

Nancy's husband adds that the openness allowed him to feel more comfortable as a parent in processing their children's needs. He also felt that the openness allowed the people involved in the situation to also be in control of it. The birthmother knows where her baby is going, and the adoptive parents know where the baby is coming from. Adds this adoptive father, "I also think that statistically, if you're not for open adoption you're really going against the odds. More and more birthmothers are opting to select the people who they want to raise that birthchild. In our case, the birthmother was thrilled to have found a stable family environment. She felt she would not allow a child to be raised as she was raised."

Another young birthmother, whose parents were divorced, tells of choosing an open adoption after getting pregnant at age sixteen. Her mother wouldn't let her stay with her, and her father didn't think he could deal with having a child around, and she knew that she didn't want an abortion. "So my dad knew this lawyer and he said he knew this couple and my mom and I met them. They had this three-year-old son who was adopted and I thought it was pretty neat how they all got along. We asked them a lot of questions we'd prepared beforehand, like how they'd discipline him and stuff like that. They were like my parents' age, I think. And we saw each other while I was pregnant, like we went to the zoo and out to McDonald's, stuff like that. She came to the hospital, too, when I gave birth, and then I signed the papers I had to, and now she's got the kid and I can't believe how lucky I am! If I want to know how he's doing I can write or even phone her. And right now I'm still in school and I'm trying to get my driver's license. I think it would have been really hard to just give him up and never know what happened to him."

For some triads, open adoption is proving to be very successful. Yet not every open adoption works, and not every birthparent opts for it. Becky, a woman who placed a baby boy ten years ago when she was nineteen, had no desire to choose the adoptive parents. "My feeling about that is, I didn't do such a great job of choosing a father for my child," she says. Nor did she want to meet the adoptive couple. She felt that if she couldn't raise the child herself, she would suffer seeing him raised by someone else.

Like many adoptive parents, she also believed that the child would be better off with an unconfused sense of who his parents were. Married now, and the mother of two children, Becky says that she will accept her birthson if he chooses to find her when he is an adult. She adds, "I'm going to be someone who loves him like no one else in this whole world loves him. But I'm not going to be his mother."[2]

The nonfiction book *Open Adoption*, by Lawrence Caplan, brings up a concern in open adoption.[3] It tells the story of Peggy Bass, a twenty-year-old college junior who chose to relinquish her baby in a semi-open adoption. Peggy and the baby's birthfather kept the pregnancy a secret from their parents; Peggy feared that her family would want her to keep the baby, which she claimed was not her wish. The birthfather was afraid that his father would feel he had not lived up to his high expectations. Based on her research, Peggy wanted to have some openness in the adoption so that she could know where her baby would be and the adoptive parents would know where the baby had come from. After some negative experiences with agencies, she chose an independent adoption through a lawyer.

Peggy searched for an adoptive family by looking at

ads in the classified section of her newspaper. The ad she answered had actually been written by a California lawyer, Diane Michaelsen, for six couples who were her clients. The ad told of a "happily married, financially secure couple hoping to share our love, our lives, and our future with an infant."

As it turned out, most of the adoptions arranged by Michaelsen involved a meeting between the birthmother and the adoptive couple; many involved some continuing contact between the two parties through pictures and letters; and some of them resulted in lasting relationships through phone calls and visits.

Peggy met the adoptive parents, visited their home, and even stayed with them. After she gave birth to "Rebecca," the baby was relinquished right on schedule. Afterwards, Peggy and the birthfather came to see Rebecca. Then the adoptive couple believed that they were on their own, but would continue some form of contact with Peggy, who they liked and wished well. They had been led to believe that Peggy would someday marry the birthfather and they marveled at how well she had everything under control and at the maturity she had shown throughout the situation. Although they had always had some fear that Peggy might back out at the last moment and take the baby back, things had seemed to go smoothly.

In reality, Peggy was not being totally honest with the adoptive parents or with herself. Finally, the strain of her secret proved too great. She ran away to Florida, and when she came back the next day, she told her parents the truth about consenting to adoption, broke up with her boyfriend, went into counseling, and decided not to see the adoptive parents until she was ready to resume contact.

Since Peggy had changed so dramatically, Rebecca's adoptive parents feared that she would demand the baby back. To protect themselves, they chose to have no contact with her except what was necessary to legalize the documents that would finalize the adoption. Cases like this one lead people like William Pierce, president of the National Committee for Adoption, a Washington umbrella group for 141 agencies, to maintain that open adoption is potentially risky and harmful. The irreconcilable difference between traditional adoption and open adoption, as Pierce and many adoptive parents see it, is the sense of entitlement to be a full and independent adoptive parent versus sharing that responsibility with the birthparent(s). Those who support open adoption say that, for the adoptee, open adoption leads to clarity, and closed adoption leads to confusion about who one's "real" parents are.

In a pilot study of seventeen adoptive families and birthparents done by Ruth G. McRoy and her colleagues at the University of Texas, the results indicate that "given the balance of the risks and values of openness in adoption, the greatest benefit and the least risk seem to occur in families with semi-open adoptions."[4]

It should be noted that birthparent activists point out that arrangements for open adoption are not legally enforceable. Once the adoption is final, the birthparents have no legal rights. As Jim Gritter, child-welfare supervisor of the Community Family and Children's Service adoption agency in Traverse City, Michigan, reports, open adoption is "a gigantic exercise in trust. It's a gentleman's agreement."[5]

AGENCY
VERSUS
INDEPENDENT
ADOPTIONS

As soon as a young woman decides to place a baby for adoption, or even considers the option, what is her next step? How does she go about finding the best adoptive parents for her child? How does she handle her own mixed emotions during this traumatic period?

Adoptions are basically handled through agencies or through independent or private facilitators. Independent adoptions may take place when birthparents and adoptive parents locate each other through a lawyer, an obstetrician, or even a nonprofessional. Thirty-seven states allow facilitators and intermediaries. In the remaining states they are not legal.

There are pros and cons to both agency and independent adoptions. Supporters of independent adoptions consider them a clever way to circumvent public and private agencies, which often have many rules, restrictions, and long waits. However, critics of independent adoptions call them a risky way to find a baby. They claim that agencies do a much better job than lawyers in carefully screening adoptive parents and counseling the birthparent(s) so that everyone involved can have peace of mind and the child can have the best chance at a happy, healthy life.

▲ THE AGENCY APPROACH

Janet Dawes, of the Arizona Children's Home (ACH), feels that the agency approach is best because the birthmother's interest is better represented. Each birthmother who comes to the ACH is counseled to make a decision in her own best interest. The ACH will help her even if she decides to raise the child rather than consent to adoption. Ms. Dawes indicates that in this period women are very vulnerable and can easily be swayed in their decisions.

Like the ACH, many agencies have extensive programs for adoptive parents. By the time couples (or single men and women) complete them, they are sure about the kind of adoption they can handle, and the agency feels secure enough about them to present their file to a birthmother or birthparents. A good agency will also want to be sure that both spouses in a couple want to adopt, and that the couple doesn't want to adopt for the wrong reasons, for instance, to hold a marriage together. While public agencies concentrate on special-needs children, private agencies remain the traditional vehicle for finding healthy infants. However, private agencies may also have other specialties, including special-needs children or foreign adoptions. Private agencies can be either nonprofit or for-profit.

Some private agencies are restricted to one religion, others are not. The largest adoption agency in the United States is Bethany Christian Services. It has fifty offices in twenty-seven states, annually places over a thousand children, young people, and infants for adoption, and accepts children and adoptive parents of all religions.

Although public agencies often do not have a fee or have only a minimal one, private agencies do. This fee, which can be set or can be on a sliding scale, generally begins at around $8,000 for a nonprofit agency adoption and can run as high as $15,000 to $20,000 and more for an infant adoption. Catholic Services in Tucson uses a sliding scale that is usually 10 percent of the couple's gross income. Some critics complain that the fees keep minority families from adopting.

Agencies generally have several qualifications for potential adoptive parents to meet. They may be looking for couples who have medical documents proving their infertility. They may also require couples to be married a specific length of time and to be no older or younger than a certain age.

As mentioned earlier, the ACH Infant Program begins with an orientation meeting at which potential adoptive parents receive a general idea of the agency's commitment to open adoption. The ACH will not accept any couples who will not participate in an adoption that is at least semi-open. While other agencies represent only closed adoptions, today most customarily craft adoption plans based on the desires and needs of birthparents.

After the ACH orientation meetings, potential adoptive parents who find the agency's approach and fees acceptable are invited to fill out an application for future orientations. These will be part of the extensive home study that will enable them to be certified to adopt by Arizona, since the ACH abides by state standards and regulations.

The ACH has recently begun having potential adoptive parents write a letter to the birthparent. The agency believes that the personality of the couple comes across better through letter writing than in an application form, thus making for better matches. In an open adoption, the birthmother reviews the files to see if any of the applications appeal to her. Then, if she and the adoptive parents agree, they will meet each other.

At many agencies, birthmothers receive one or more sessions of counseling, depending upon their needs and desires as well as state regulations. The counselors at the ACH realize that this is a difficult time for the birthmother since she has already bonded to the child she is carrying. They help her express her feelings, learn what to expect, and think through what she is doing. They also help the birthmother decide what will go into the adoptee's book, which she prepares to give to the adoptive parents who will in turn give it to the child. Perhaps she will want to include a personal letter, perhaps pictures of herself. The ACH works to counsel everyone in the adoption triad on an ongoing basis. Like many other agencies, it also provides support groups for birthmothers, children, and adoptive parents. Finally, if the birthfather is involved, he, too, can get counseling through the ACH.

At their best, agencies can be caring places where adoptive parents as well as birthparents receive the kind of warmth and nurturing they need during this time, a time that will probably be highly charged emotionally.

▲ THE INDEPENDENT APPROACH

The alternative to agency adoptions—independent, or private, adoptions—allow birthparents to bypass the agencies and place their babies directly with adoptive parents. To give you an idea of how greatly state laws differ on private adoptions, in 1991 independent placements were not allowed by state law in Connecticut, Delaware, Massachusetts, Michigan, and North Dakota.[1] In California, 80 percent of all adoptions are arranged through lawyers, independently of agencies. And, according to the National Committee for Adoption, about half of the healthy infants in the United States are now placed independently.[2]

There are several main reasons for choosing an independent adoption. Birthparents may desire more control over the situation than they feel their local agencies can provide. They may want to select the adoptive parents, talk to them, and even meet them, but the agencies in their area are not responsive to their request. (Agencies may allow "identified adoptions," which were mentioned earlier. In these adoptions, the birthparent and adoptive parent(s) meet outside the agency setting. After this, they use the agency's services to formalize the adoption.) Financial needs may also be a factor in the birthmother's decision. Many agencies cannot pay medical bills or other expenses, although they may be able to help a woman receive public assistance and other forms of help. Or, like independent placements, they may be able to arrange for the adoptive parents to pay for reasonable expenses.

A birthmother may also be reluctant to seek out an agency because she wants to avoid going through counseling. She may fear being questioned or being judged by the agency for becoming pregnant or for consenting to adopt. She may also not want to confront her feelings about her situation.

Adoptive parents who choose an independent adoption may do so for a variety of reasons. They may be people who have been rejected by agencies they've applied to. In some cases, this could be due to the length of their marriage, their religion, their age, or a physical handicap one or the other has. In other cases, rejection could come about because a social worker feels that they are not suitable to be parents. Sometimes a personality clash with a social worker can result in a rejection.

Then, too, a couple may choose an independent placement because they do not want to wait for their local agency to find an infant for them, which may take over three years. Independent adoptions often produce faster results. In one study conducted in California, all but 2 of 105 infants were placed in their adoptive homes within a year of their parents' starting to investigate independent adoption.[3] Another reason an independent adoption may be favored is simply because a couple may hear of a pregnant woman willing to place her child for adoption in this way.

All adoptions require legal services. In agency adoptions, the lawyer is provided by the agency. In independent adoptions, a lawyer may initiate the process; if not, a lawyer has to be hired. Generally, it is not advisable for the same lawyer to represent both the birthmother and the adoptive parents.

ADOPTION–AN OPTION FOR YOU AND YOUR BABY: If you would like your child to be raised in a loving, caring, financially secure family environment –please call us collect. Medical/legal expenses pd. Nancy & Mike, 000-000-0000.

ADOPT. Answer our prayers. Happily married couple will provide lots of love, good education & warm loving country home for baby. Legal & confidential. Call collect, 000-000-0000.

ADOPTION is a loving choice for you and your newborn. We can provide a warm, happy, secure home. Expenses paid. Confidential. Call Fran & Jay collect, 000-000-0000.

ADOPTION. Loving couple wishes to adopt precious newborn to shower with lots of affection. Medical expenses paid. Please call collect, 000-000-0000.

ADOPTION Empty nursery waiting for a baby. Loving couple longs to become father and full-time mother. Please let our dream come true. Expenses paid. Call Marie & Pat collect, 000-000-0000.

Several different scenarios can take place. A birthmother may seek out a lawyer to help her find a referral. The lawyer may know of someone or may ask other lawyers for the latest list of couples seeking to adopt. In another scenario, the birthmother may find the adoptive parents on her own and then seek a lawyer's services to help finalize the agreement. The search for an independent adoption could start with a birthmother reading ads in the personal column of her local or college newspaper. In states where adoption advertising is legal (nineteen states forbid it), the ads may be placed by potential adoptive couples themselves or by the lawyer representing them. Often, the ads include a toll-free number or invite the applicants to call collect.

Birthparents have found that advertisements aren't the only source of information about potential adoptive parents. Obstetricians, as well as officials or members of one's place of worship, may also supply leads. Birthparents may even find potential adoptive parents through word of mouth. In one case, the birthmother's mother had a lawyer who happened to overhear a couple at a cocktail party talk about wanting to adopt. "Excuse me," he said, "but I'm a lawyer and I know of someone who is going to have a baby she wants to place." The couple's eyes lit up, and a new adoption story began.

As for cost, the price of an ordinary private adoption is not much higher than that of an agency adoption, and in some cases it may be about the same. In New York, for instance, the total cost for legal, medical, advertising, telephone, and travel expenses is typically $8,000 to $12,000. However, this amount can soar if there are medical complications.

Like agency adoptions, independent adoptions require a home study. However, it is done through the court system. Agencies claim that these home studies are not as thorough as are agency home studies. In Arizona, the home study is done through the Juvenile Court and generally consists of a home visit, one office interview before the child is placed, a reference check, and a second office interview after placement. The court, unlike an adoption agency, is not responsible for the child or for actually placing him or her.

Other states may not even require home studies in independent adoptions. The most notorious case in recent years of an independent adoption gone wrong was that of Lisa Steinberg, a six-year-old girl who was beaten to death by Joel Steinberg, the New York lawyer who illegally kept the girl after promising her birthmother to arrange an adoption. At that time, a home study was required only for infants born out of state. Since 1989, however, a New York State ruling requires a home study for anyone who takes custody of an infant. The ruling also forbids any lawyer from representing both the birthmother and the adoptive parents.

William Pierce, president of the National Committee for Adoption, believes that abuses have multiplied as formal agencies have lost control of the adoption process. He urges stricter regulation of independent adoptions.[4] And some organizations, including the Child Welfare League of America, would prohibit independent adoptions altogether.[5] One of the harshest criticisms agencies have about independent adoption is that the birthmothers often receive no counseling.

But this may not always be the case. Deborah Pratte, a Tucson, Arizona, lawyer who specializes in family law, has represented the birthmothers in several adoptions. She explained that in her experience, the potential adoptive parents pay the necessary medical costs for the birthmother, which includes counseling if the birthmother chooses to have it. "Most of the clients I've seen have been really open to counseling," says Ms. Pratte, "and every one of the adoptive parents I've seen has been happy to pay for it."

However, in any adoption, agency or independent, it is illegal for money to be paid for the child or given to the birthmother as a gift. The court requires an accounting that includes everything the birthmother receives to pay her medical expenses, and possibly her living expenses as well as her maternity clothes.

Independent adoption is sometimes criticized on the grounds that once a birthmother has had her medical bills paid, she will find it that much harder to back out of the arrangement should she change her mind. On the other hand, the money potential adoptive parents spend on the birthmother before her delivery is no guarantee that she will relinquish the child. And money spent cannot be recovered if she does have a change of heart. Add to this the emotional trauma suffered, and independent adoption can be very expensive, indeed.

> "I thought I could do it until I had the baby. When I saw him, I couldn't stand the thought of someone else bringing him up, of me never seeing him again or not until he wanted to see me. I knew they [the adoptive parents] spent a lot of money and don't think I'm not grateful. Maybe someday I can pay them back. It's just that . . . I had no idea how I'd feel until I saw that baby. That made the whole thing so much more real to me. Hopefully, there won't be a next time, but if there is, I'll be much more honest with myself."
>
> —J. R., a single birthmother who is now bringing up her son

Like many other adoption lawyers, Ms. Pratte will handle open or closed adoptions, depending on the wishes of the people involved. She has found that some birthmothers as well as adoptive parents want the adoptions to be completely confidential. In other cases, where birthmothers and potential adoptive parents select an open adoption, Ms. Pratte has the latter submit a letter, sometimes with pictures, giving detailed explanations of why they want to adopt a child. She gives the document(s) to the birthmother to use as a basis for her choice, and will sometimes submit letters from several different couples to a birthmother if necessary. If none of the candidates interests the

48

birthmother, Ms. Pratte continues to look further. "She [the birthmother] absolutely needs to feel comfortable," says Ms. Pratte.

If the people want a meeting, Ms. Pratte arranges one. Sometimes the meeting takes place before the birth, but when the couple lives out of state, a meeting often isn't possible until after the baby is born. At meetings, there are usually two lawyers present, one representing the birthmother and the other representing the adoptive parents.

When these meetings take place after delivery, Ms. Pratte attends them with mixed feelings, since it is such a difficult time for the birthmother, yet a joyous time for the adoptive parents. "It's sad to watch someone suffering for something they're doing out of love, and then a half hour later you may be there with the adoptive parents who have been waiting for a child for fifteen years and this is the happiest moment of their lives," she says.

Although independent adoptions get their fair share of criticism from members of the adoption community, Deborah Pratte believes that in many cases they work very well. Evidence that people feel positively about her role in independent adoption comes, she believes, from the fact that she does not need to advertise except in the yellow pages as a family law attorney. Requests from birthmothers come to her by referral, through people in the community.

Finally, it is important to remember that there have been, and continue to be, adoption malpractices and scams conducted by both agencies and independent facilitators. These are sometimes possible because regulations are not strict enough or well enough enforced.

Perhaps the deciding factor for birthmothers is to choose an agency or independent facilitator with whom they feel a sense of trust. And, judging from the diverse opinions about them, neither road to adoption appears to be the unequivocal "best way to go."

TRANSRACIAL ADOPTIONS

"As a black man raised by a white couple, I know that my parents didn't pick up the signs of racism in my community. They thought everything was just fine. But it wasn't. I think the only way you can adopt a child from another race is if you make sure you help your kids treasure their birth culture and even then, I'm not so sure it works."

—Thirty-year-old black male adoptee

"I was raised in a white family, and as far as I can see, it's only done me good, because I feel more accepting of other people. I don't see any self-image problems. I like myself."

—Eighteen-year-old black female adoptee

One of today's most heated debates among adoption experts and adoptive families concerns transracial and cross-cultural adoptions, the placing of a child of one race or culture in a family of another race or culture. This is a very sensitive issue with critics strongly claiming that such adoptions are ill advised, although recent studies indicate that they also have great merit.

Those opposed to transracial adoptions—whether black/white, Native American/non-Native American, or Asian/non-Asian—say that the children's basic identity becomes diluted, and, as a result, they suffer from dangerously low self-esteem. The most vocal critic of transracial adoption is the National Association of Black Social Workers (NABSW). This group has called such matches "cultural genocide."[1] According to the association, only a black family can prepare a black child to live in a society in which racial prejudice must be confronted on a daily basis. As the black director of a foster care agency said on a recent television show addressing this issue, "What you don't get is the nuances."

Critics like Robie Littles, a former vice president of the NABSW, believe that it is not enough to teach a black child about his or her culture by going to the library or attending classes in African-American history. As Littles puts it, "It's more a matter of what [black people] go through every day, all our lives. There's stuff that your parents, grandparents, teach you, tricks of the trade, street knowledge to survive in a racist society. The do's and don'ts. Real-life teaching . . . In spite of [adoptive parents'] benevolence, they just have not walked the walk."

Littles fears that black children raised by white parents might become racial dropouts. "When a black kid says, 'I consider myself a human being,' that's cultural genocide. Anytime a person denies what he or she is, their race has lost one individual."[2]

▲ THE MODERN HISTORY OF TRANSRACIAL ADOPTIONS

Transracial adoptions had been relatively rare before 1960. But by 1971, one-third of all black children being adopted were placed with white families. This is attributed primarily to the introduction of the birth control pill in the 1960s, and to the civil rights movement, which helped change attitudes about racial segregation. Adopting across racial lines seemed to some to be in the spirit of integration.[3]

Yet, as a result of the NABSW's opposition, which was especially strong in the early 1970s, many restrictions were placed on black-white adoptions. At least thirty-five states now have regulations requiring social workers to work as hard as possible to place children with parents of the same race. Transracial adoptions of all kinds dropped from a high of 2,540 in 1971 to less than half that number in recent years.[4]

In all, an estimated 25,000 black children have been adopted by whites in the United States. Meanwhile, the association's position on the subject remains unchanged.

▲ ADOPTION BARRIERS FOR MINORITY PARENTS

Today, the adoption community appears to be in agreement that the preferred match unites children with an adoptive family of the same racial and cultural background. However, there are other realities to consider. For instance, there are many more adoptable nonwhite babies than white ones. At the same time, there are fewer minority families than non-minority families who either wish to or are being allowed to adopt. A 1987 government study shows that there are five times as many minority children in the adoption system as there are potential adoptive minority families. That study also found that among prospective minority adoptees there are three times as many older and physically and mentally challenged children as there are young, healthy ones.[5]

According to some adoption specialists, minority parents are kept out of the adoption arena because of current adoption practices. They may find that they are turned down by agencies because they are single, over forty, or have modest incomes. Yet, in the black community, many households are headed by single parents over forty years of age who live on modest incomes. The critics say that the adoption community is denying children a right to a life-style that is part of their culture.

The Institute for Black Parenting (IBP) in Los Angeles, California, readily accepts single parents, and in some cases considers them the "placement of choice." The goal of this agency is to empower black families. To that end, they make sure that the social worker assigned to potential adoptive parents is one familiar with African-American culture. In the first twenty months of the agency's life, 2,500 black families inquired about adoption, 400 families were studied, and 110 children were placed.[6]

California has a statewide television campaign that urges African Americans and Hispanics to consider adoption. In Brooklyn, New York, a nonprofit agency called the Miracle Makers has placed 671 children in 473 black foster homes during the past two years by recruiting foster parents at churches, civic centers, and homes. The agency then asked the families if they would consider adoption; 125 families replied that they would. To date, reports the agency's deputy executive director, Eddie Lacewell, thirty-seven of these adoptions have been finalized.

The search for black families to adopt has also led to kinship programs in which relatives of children in foster care or ready for adoption are tracked down and asked to consider adopting the child. In many cases, the child is already in the home, and state laws allow home studies and other requirements to be more lenient than for "stranger" placements.

Supporters of transracial adoption claim that it is a workable alternative, especially if the children are removed from foster homes in which they have no permanency and are placed in loving homes where they have a better chance to become well-adjusted. This stand is supported by a twenty-year research study by sociologist Rita Simon of American University in Washington, D.C., and Howard Altstein of the University of Maryland. The study, which began in 1972, indicates that children generally do well with adoptive parents of another race and that "transracial adoption causes no special problems. In fact, it may produce adults who possess superior interpersonal skills and talents."[7]

The study involved 386 black children and the 204 white families that had adopted them. Two interviewers, one black and one white, visited each home. One interviewer talked to the parents, the other to the birthchildren and adoptees. The group was assessed in 1979 and again in 1983–84.

The study found that once the adoptees were in school, they had both white and black friends. They had more black friends than their white brothers and sisters, but their white siblings had more black friends than most white children. When it came to dating, the study showed that the black adoptees dated whites and blacks in equal numbers; 75 percent of their white siblings dated whites exclusively and 25 percent dated either blacks exclusively or both whites and blacks. As far as educational achievement, teen pregnancy, and other issues, the African-American children "resemble white averages," says Simon. "Most of these kids grew up in middle-class families. They resemble black middle-class families also."[8]

According to Dr. Simon, transracial adoption works best when families understand society's racism as experienced by the child, while at the same time respecting and preserving their children's heritage and working at truly becoming a multicultural family.

While the researchers do not claim that transracial adoption is better than racially matched adoption, their findings indicate that such matches can produce emotionally healthy children who are comfortable with their racial identity and are close to their parents.

Another study that supports interracial adoptions was conducted at the University of Texas. Researchers studied two groups of thirty African-American middle-class adolescents, one group adopted by black families, the other by white families. They concluded that there were no major differences in the adoptees' levels of self-esteem, although the way they perceived their racial identities differed slightly. Those raised in black families were more likely to date and be open to marrying other blacks, while those with white parents tended to dismiss or deny racial differences. Her findings have led the chief researcher, Ruth McRoy, to recommend that the first preference in transracial adoptions be given to white adoptive parents who have ties to the black community, live in integrated neighborhoods, and send their birthchildren to integrated schools.[9]

Although the results of these studies speak well of interracial matches, groups such as the NABSW insist that a greater effort should be made by adoption and child-welfare agencies to recruit minority families to adopt. Morris Jeff, the president of the NABSW, continues to maintain that barriers such as income and housing requirements are used to exclude minority families from adoption.

In practice, most states today give preference to racial and cultural matches. They will also look for religious matches when requested by birthparents and/or adoptive parents. In some cases, the birthparents may request a family that will not force a particular religion on a child. Some agencies will delay a transracial adoption in order to find a racial match. However, this adds to the disproportionate number of black children already awaiting adoption. In Massachusetts, a state with a 5 percent black population, 60 percent of the children on the state adoption register are black.[10] This situation has led concerned social workers to allow transracial adoptions, especially for handicapped and other difficult-to-place children. And throughout the country, state and local groups continue developing and fine-tuning programs to increase the number of minority adoptive parents.

▲ NATIVE AMERICAN ADOPTIONS

For Native American children, problems continue despite the fact that they come under the jurisdiction of the 1978 Indian Child Welfare Act (ICWA). The Act was passed to curb the great number of Indian children then being adopted into white families. During the 1960s and early 1970s, one in six Indian children were raised in a white home. Some smaller tribes lost up to one third of their children in this way. Later, as Native Americans became more vocal in determining their own policies, and began developing their land and mineral resources, they became increasingly concerned about their greatest natural resource—their children.[11]

At first, the ICWA seemed to be the solution to a major problem. Basically, it gives tribal courts the power to make custody and foster-care decisions for children considered legal residents of a reservation. It states that every effort must be made to place the child with an Indian family, even one from another tribe, over a white family. Supporters say that the Act is helping to keep Indian families together and is preserving Indian cultural and tribal integrity so that Indian children grow up with a sense of their racial and ethnic identity.

Critics of the Act say that it is not working well at all. Carol Locust, from the Native American Research and Training Center at the University of Arizona, points out the "good faith clause." In order for the Act to work, state officials have to recognize the sovereignty of the Indian nation. Since some states do not want to recognize the sovereignty of any Indian nation, they do not abide by it, she says.

According to Ms. Locust, Indian children are a premium both for foster placement and adoption into non-Indian homes. "To the sovereign Indian nations, Indian adoptions into non-Indian homes is another type of genocide," she says. Ms. Locust believes that the setup for tribal genocide works like this: for various reasons, Indian children are taken from Indian families by a state agency, which places them in non-Indian families without notifying the tribes until the very last moment. (According to the ICWA the tribe is supposed to be notified within twenty-four hours of the state agency taking the child in, so a foster home can be found for that child within the tribe.) Then, says Ms. Locust, the state agency complains of how cruel it is to yank a child out of a secure and loving home and force him or her to live with strangers. According to Ms. Locust, "We lose more of our tribal members to this blatant type of expatriation than we ever lost to smallpox."

Ms. Locust has been called to speak in several Native American adoption trials because she has compiled eight years of informal research on how their adoption affects Native American children. She has placed ads in Indian publications, asking for replies from Native Americans adopted into white homes. She says that her studies show that "Indian adults who were placed in non-Indian homes as children have an extremely high rate of psychological problems, a great number of suicides, and a stress rate that is greater than that of prisoners of war . . . Most of them are angry, and all of them grieve constantly over the loss of their true families and their cultural heritage."

According to Ms. Locust, every one of the adult Indians who responded to her questions said that they knew they were different before they ever entered grade school, and by the time they were in high school, they knew they had to find their families and their tribe. Yet, when they reached their goal, they discovered that their lack of knowledge about their language, culture, and families made them feel lost in their true culture, as well as in their adopted one. Ms. Locust says that time and again she has heard Native American adoptees wonder why the birthmother didn't keep them and let them help her in some way.

To Ms. Locust, the most hurtful thing that's come through in the letters she has received is that the adoptees felt that they had "no mirror image, no reflection back to them of who they were. There were always these white faces and they were always searching, searching, searching for someone to identify with."

Ms. Locust explains that as a Native American, in addition to tribal heritage you have certain tribal rights, and if you are denied this you are missing a great deal. But there is another important issue to consider for Native Americans. In many tribes, children are born into particular religious roles in the community. "When you start removing these people like we have for the last fifty years, think of all the holes in the fabric of our community and think of the loss in our religious belief systems."

Ms. Locust considers Native American adoptees as adults of two worlds. With that in mind, she encourages her fellow American Indians to welcome them back, and work with them, "for they are ours and we cherish them. We try to replace for them all the teachings and rituals they missed when they were young, but that is not always possible."

She suggests that if a Native American mother can't take care of the child, the father should be the first choice as caretaker. Then, if the child can't be with either of them, other relatives should be the next choice. If not relatives, then place the child with the tribe. If not with the tribe, then certainly in an Indian home, "So they can look at somebody else who has a brown face," she says.

Ms. Locust suggests that the state should provide adequate funding for social workers to intensively recruit for adoptive homes in Indian communities. Ms. Locust would also like to see funds provided for state workers to cooperate with tribal ICWA offices in locating extended family members, and fulfilling ICWA rules that require states to inform tribes of problems before, not after, Indian children are placed in foster homes.

Meanwhile, critics of the ICWA say that it is too restrictive, that it does not always serve the best interests of Native American children and the wishes of some Indian mothers, who would prefer their children not live on the reservation. "I've lived on the reservation. There's nothing there. I want my baby to have a better life," said Patricia Keetso. A Navajo woman, Keetso herself had been placed in a white home as a child. She wanted a white couple from California to adopt her daughter Allyssa. However, the tribe took Allyssa, then nine months old, away from both her and the adoptive parents and returned the child to the reservation. The Navajo court eventually gave the white couple permanent custody, and also ordered them to involve Allyssa with her natural family and culture.[12]

If experts can agree on anything, it is that there are not enough Indian families to adopt all the Indian children in foster care; Indian children continue to be placed in foster care at almost four times the rate of non-Indian children.

Alcoholism among Indian parents remains a major reason for children being removed from the home. According to some estimates, as many as 25 percent of Indian children may be affected by fetal alcohol syndrome, which hampers normal physical and mental development. Surely this, some argue, is as great a threat to Indian culture and life as white adoption. If loving, white homes are available, they ask, isn't that better than leaving a child with an abusive natural parent or in the limbo of foster care?

Even deeper than the quality of life issue is the question of who decides. American non-Indian women generally have the right to determine where their children are placed, but Native American women, because they are citizens of separate Indian nations, are not protected by the U.S. Constitution. Their right to self-determination is balanced against the tribe's right to perpetuate itself.

William Pierce, of the National Committee for Adoption, originally campaigned for the ICWA. Today, he says that it is being used in ways he never intended, for example, to thwart voluntary adoptions of infants. According to Mr. Pierce, there are cases in which Indian women, and white women impregnated by Indian men, have had abortions rather than fight the tribe over placement of the baby. He believes that the ICWA discriminates against the non-Indian part of a child's heritage by permitting Indian courts jurisdiction over children who are in some cases only one-eighth Indian. However, the tribal courts insist that they do not automatically give the child to an Indian family, and that the outcome of certain cases supports that contention.

Janet Dawes of ACH recently attended a very moving out-of-doors placement at a Tucson, Arizona, park. The birthmother, who is Native American, and the father, who is white, composed a blessing which the birthmother gave as she handed the baby to the adoptive parents, who are white. The ceremony was videotaped and photographed by the adoptive parents. But, before this could take place, the adoption agency made sure to follow the ICWA guidelines very carefully, because they will not work with any situation unless they get tribal clearance. There is no doubt that serious grievances must be addressed here, but for now it would seem that each case must be evaluated on its own.

▲ FOREIGN ADOPTION

Although recent attempts by white families to adopt black children have stirred strong emotions in supporters and critics alike, another type of transracial and cross-cultural adoption has been going on for decades. That is the adoption of foreign children, particularly of Asian ancestry, by white families. For several years, large numbers of children from Korea, Taiwan, the Philippines, and India have been adopted by white American families. Recently, adoptions of children from eastern Europe and South America have been rising.

In general, although foreign adoptions are becoming more difficult than they were in the past, many prospective adoptive parents find them an attractive alternative to adopting local children. Parents, or singles in some cases, may be motivated to adopt from foreign countries because there aren't enough local children available to them. The potential parents may fail to meet agency requirements, although they are actually fine candidates for parenting. For instance, foreign agencies may be willing to allow adoption by single parents or families with other children when many local agencies will not consider them. People who don't wish to wait for an American adoption also may choose to take their love outside the United States, to countries where it may take only two years to adopt a child, instead of three to six or more.

In the past, South Korea was the prime source of foreign adoptions. This is now changing. In response to criticism that it was abandoning its children to foreigners, the South Korean government began heavily promoting birth control and encouraging Korean families to adopt. As a result of its successful programs, the adoption rate by foreigners has dropped considerably. The ultimate goal of the reduction is to bring the rate of adoption by foreigners to close to zero in that country.[13]

South Korea's policies have increased the demand for available children from Latin America, eastern Europe, and elsewhere. Yet, wherever they originate, foreign adoptions have always been controversial. For the most part, they are handled legitimately, and good matches are made.

However, there have been cases in which children are matched with inadequate parents or are even sold. Reported incidents include El Salvadoran and Mexican children being kidnapped and sold to American parents.

In Romania, for a brief period after the end of a harsh governmental regime during which adoption was illegal, the country had many institutions filled with young children. This situation led to an open sale of babies to American, Canadian, and Western European adoptive parents who paid for them with cash, as well as with material goods such as cars. As one hopeful adoptive mother from the United States said, some people who went to Romania to buy babies did not think about the ethics involved. On the contrary, they felt that "what they're getting and what they're giving the child in the end justifies what they do to get the child."[14] Many of these children turned out to be not only illegally obtained, but also unhealthy, suffering from AIDS and the Hepatitis B virus. In an effort to avoid abuses of the system, United States regulations for foreign adoptions have become stricter. The Romanian government has also tightened its own regulations. Both steps have led to fewer adoptions from Romania. This is a familiar pattern that has been repeated in other countries—lenient rules lead to abuses that are eventually curtailed or eradicated by making the process of adoption by foreigners more difficult.

Today, foreign adoptions involve a great deal of red tape. The United States Immigration and Naturalization Service (INS) explains that its tough laws are designed first and foremost to protect children. Would-be parents of foreign adoptees must pass state requirements, as well as receive FBI and state fingerprint clearance. Then they must be approved by the child's native country, as well as the INS, whose approval is necessary before the United States State Department will issue an immigration visa.

The federal immigration law mandates that one parent must be at least twenty-five years of age, but the foreign country may require one parent to be even older. For instance, Thailand requires one parent to be at least thirty years of age, and China requires thirty-five as the minimum age to adopt, both countries believing that the older the parent, the wiser. But the Philippines seeks younger adoptive parents because they are accustomed to their population dying at a much younger age.

Avoiding the Risks of Foreign Adoption ▲ In the United States, foreign adoption is possible through a local agency, a nonlocal agency that runs an intercountry adoption program, or through a facilitator or intermediary. A facilitator could be, for instance, a social worker in the United States who works with an attorney in another country. Direct placements are also possible, with the potential adoptive parent(s) traveling to the child's country of origin and dealing directly with an orphanage that places newborn infants. While many facilitators are honest, some are not, and will take a client's money without helping to obtain a child, or will charge much more than is necessary.

One way to minimize the risks is to work with a licensed United States organization that has established a relationship with, and has legitimate contacts in, foreign countries. Mary Lee Schupp is the founder and director of Hand in Hand International, an organization that has been handling foreign adoptions since 1974. She says that her staff looks for families who have plenty of love to give a child, as well as a lack of prejudice against other races, because they're going to have to be a stronghold for their children so that they can feel good about who they are. "You can't whitewash a foreign child very easily or pretend that they're your birthchild, so you have to deal with cultural and interracial issues," she reminds prospective adoptive parents.

Hand in Hand requires parents or singles to go through a very rigorous screening process. They have a group session, then a home study at which the agency delves into their background. In addition, they must go through the state certification process and approval by the FBI and the immigration department. They must also meet the guidelines of the child's country. For instance, the Philippines will only allow adoption by two-parent families, so an application from a single parent would not be submitted there.

However, many foreign countries do consider single adoptive parents. These include Brazil, El Salvador, Honduras, Peru, and Bolivia. Most require that a single adopter be at least twenty-five years old. Singles and other adoptive parents must remember that the rules for foreign adoptions are very changeable; a country may accept single adopters one year and close its doors to them the next. For that reason, Betsy Burch, Director of Single Parents Adopting Children Everywhere (SPACE), a Massachusetts support group, advises singles to adopt siblings so they get two children at the same time, before requirements change.[15]

As one expert reports, it is ironic that while there are literally millions of foreign children without families, only a small percentage are available for adoption. An estimated 100,000 children are living on the streets in Bogota, Colombia, but until these children get into the adoption system, typically by entering an orphanage, respectable adoption agencies will not work with them.

To avoid abuses in the system, agencies such as Hand in Hand only deal with the governments in foreign countries or with attorneys approved by them. Hand in Hand also does not allow families to get a copy of their home study and take it to a foreign country, because if they did, they might bypass the agency attorney. As Ms. Schupp explains, "Everything is done prior to their going so it knocks out the potential for abuse."

There have also been rumors about abuses on this end, including the one about Americans and Europeans adopting children from Third World countries in order to provide organ transplants for waiting children in the United States. To counter such claims, Hand in Hand sends back reports and pictures so that the foreign governments they are working with can see how well the children are doing. Hand in Hand also puts together a book for the foreign country with pictures and letters so officials there can see that the adoptees are thriving. And when foreign government people come to the States, Hand in Hand arranges for them to visit the adoptees' homes. Ms. Schupp feels that this is also good for the children because it puts them in contact with people from their homelands.

The cost for a foreign adoption varies depending on the foreign country's program. According to the National Adoption Information Clearinghouse, it can range anywhere from $10,000 to $20,000, making it comparable in price to adoptions through private and nonprofit agencies in the United States. Open adoption is sometimes not a possibility in foreign adoptions, especially with infants given up at birth by mothers who went to the hospital under a fictitious name and address and can't be traced. But in some countries it is very much a possibility.

Countering the Critics ▲ Critics of foreign adoptions feel that there are plenty of children available in the United States. They also worry that a child's native culture will be neglected as the child grows up far from its homeland. Susan Cox, director of development for Holt International, a child welfare and adoption agency in Eugene, Oregon, believes that while ethnicity and culture are extremely important in looking at the well-being of the child, his or her best interests are met by having a family to provide nurturing.

Cox is herself an adoptee, having come to this country in 1956 as the 167th Korean child to be adopted in the United States. Although her family embraced her culture, she acknowledged in the newspaper *The Christian Science Monitor* that she always wondered what her mother looked like and what her children would look like.[16] She recalls that when she was a child, people would say that adoptees like her were delightful children, but questioned what would happen when they grew up—who would marry them, who would give them jobs? "But fifty thousand of us later, I think we've proven that the process works," she says.

Since 1956, Holt has found U.S. homes for about 30,000 Korean children. Like most agencies that arrange international adoptions, Holt has programs to help adoptees learn of the culture in which they were born. Holt International runs Heritage Camps each summer for a group of nine-to fifteen-year-old adoptees from foreign countries. The children get to see kids who look like they do, sometimes for the first time.

Hand in Hand provides support groups for the children and the parents. At the group meetings they serve foods from the various countries and show slides and films of the native countries so the children have two countries to be proud of. Hand in Hand and Holt also sponsor motherland tours back to the children's country of origin when the children become teenagers.

A Foreign Adoption that Worked ▲ Does foreign adoption work? While it remains controversial, it often works well. Ms. Schupp recently had the good fortune of leading a motherland tour back to the Philippines. On it was a young woman who began life in very unfortunate circumstances.

One day, a policeman in the Philippines saw some papers rustling in a garbage can. He thought that a rat was in the garbage, so he kicked the can. To his surprise, a little hand came out of the can. He reached in and found a baby girl. She was two-and-a-half years old, weighed only four pounds, and was blind because ants and maggots in the garbage can had eaten at her eyes. He rushed her to a Catholic orphanage, where she miraculously survived.

As it happened, a potential adoptive couple in the United States was asking for a blind child. Both the husband and wife had learned Braille and taught at a school for the blind. They felt they had the background to take care of a child who was blind. They adopted this child, and by giving her love, proper nutrition, and medical care, she thrived. Last year, at age eighteen, she returned to the Philippines on the motherland tour. A straight-A student, just out of high school, she reminded the other children, "Just listen and touch, don't just use your eyes." According to Schupp, the young woman is now attending college.

Ms. Schupp, Ms. Cox, and others advocate foreign adoption as a worthwhile alternative to growing up in an orphanage in one's native land. "A child who grows up in an orphanage is not assuming any of the benefits of that community," Ms. Cox explains. Many of the Asian, African-American, Hispanic, and Native American adopted children reaching adulthood say that the issue is not whether they were loved or appreciated but whether their adoptive parents recognized their special needs.[17] Then again, isn't that what all children want and need?

6 FOSTER CARE

> "I want to be adopted because I don't want
> to be a foster kid anymore. I hate moving to
> different houses. I like being in one choir, and
> I like being in one family. I like being in one
> church. I am doing good at home and I like
> my family.
>
> Love, Cecelia Fisher, age eight

It is estimated that some 5 million couples or individuals in
the United States want to adopt children. At the same
time, hundreds of thousands of children without permanent
homes can be found in institutions, group homes, and foster homes. Something here doesn't seem to compute unless you realize that most potential adoptive parents want
healthy white infants. The children left behind are the
"special needs" children: minorities, siblings, those with
emotional or physical challenges, and those in foster care.
According to the Child Welfare League of America, there
were about 340,000 youngsters in foster care in 1991, up
from 225,000 in the early 1980s.[1]

When children are in foster care, their biological parents retain legal custody of them and the children retain

their family's surname. In most cases, children are taken from their parents because of parental abuse or neglect and are placed in foster care by the court. In some cases, a child may enter the foster care system because the parent is unable to care for him, yet not ready to relinquish him. For instance, a teen mother may have decided to keep her baby, but when the child is one or two, the mother finds that she is unable to handle the upbringing. Rather than give the child up, she places him in foster care and tries to get her own life together before taking the child back. (This may not be an alternative in those states where foster care caseworkers are too overworked and understaffed to take on new cases.)

Foster parents are paid the cost of each foster child's clothing, housing, and food. They are also reimbursed for medical expenses, including physical and mental therapy. In total, foster parents may receive $5,000 or more a year to care for a foster child, with the ultimate plan being to return the child to the parents if that is in the child's best interests.

There are two levels of foster care, the substitute temporary family, and a special category of "therapeutic foster parents." The latter are "professional parents" who have had foster care experience and/or school-related or professional experience with children. They are recruited to help stabilize youngsters who have multiple problems. One therapeutic care parent is required to stay home full-time with the foster children, who live with them anywhere from six months to two years. The children then may return home or to a traditional foster care home, or they may become available for adoption. Sometimes the therapeutic foster home becomes a permanent place for a child who will never go home or be adopted.

▲ DANGERS IN THE "SHUTTLE SYSTEM"

In theory, and often in practice, the foster care system can be a successful way to transfer a child from a dangerous or potentially dangerous situation to one that is safe. However, foster care has many critics, including Glen Hester, head of the National Association of Former Foster Children (NAFFC) and author of the book *Days of Rage*. Mr. Hester was raised by foster parents, and although he realizes that he is virtually biting the hand that fed him, he is vocal about the major deficits he sees in the system.

According to Mr. Hester, many local and state agencies still try to reunite families that are often beyond repair. Yet when children return to their families, it often means that they lose their places in foster homes. Brenda Goldsmith, from La Hacienda, a foster care agency in Tucson, Arizona, agrees with Mr. Hester's assessment. "So what you see is a lot of children going back and forth in the system," she says. "They go back home for a while and then it doesn't work out and they come back into foster care, and the foster home they were in the first time does not have a slot available for them anymore so they go into a new foster home."

In this way, many children in the foster care system end up with multiple placements, with no sense of permanency in a safe and loving home. At each stop they may grow less hopeful and less trusting. Of the foster care caseload, nearly 60 percent have been physically and sexually abused.

In part, the birthparents may be to blame for not trying hard enough to provide a home for their children. But there is agreement among its critics that part of the problem stems from shortcomings in the social services system, since the family often does not receive the support services needed to correct whatever problems have made it fail.

The soaring number of children in foster care over the past ten years is largely attributed to parental drug abuse (crack cocaine was unheard of a decade ago). At the same time, child abuse has doubled over the past decade, and homelessness has also increased. Some social service agencies have compelled homeless parents to give up their children in order to qualify for shelter. In other cases, children leave the foster care system when they reach eighteen, only to find themselves without family or friends. This places them at risk for a life of homelessness. With caseworkers understaffed and overburdened, foster children, along with their birth families and their foster parents, have become victims of the system.

▲ HARD-TO-KEEP LAWS

In 1980, the Adoption Assistance and Child Welfare Act was passed in order to reduce foster care placements by providing services to families at risk. The law also established procedures to shorten the time that children have to stay in foster care. The law mandates that each child's case be reviewed every six months, and that a judicial hearing take place every eighteen months. Although the Act has reduced the number of children in foster care, its critics are still not satisfied with the system. Mr. Hester claims that the agencies have difficulty in conforming to federal guidelines that mandate a plan for permanent placement within eighteen months. Only about half of all foster children return home; many of the rest are suspended in a legal limbo by parents who make little effort to regain them but refuse to relinquish them fully. An absentee parent can thwart the initiation of an adoption plan if only minimal contact is maintained during the eighteen months.

As a result, most of the children in foster care are unavailable for adoption. Mr. Hester, who is a strong advocate of permanency planning for children, feels that children currently remain in the foster care system for too long. "If parents can be helped, let's help them," he says, "but there comes a time when the child has to go on with his own life." He cites an analogy in divorce cases. A man treats his wife harshly and she gets a divorce. Later, after she remarries, her first husband gets his life together. Does that mean she should terminate the second marriage and go back to her formerly abusive husband? No, says Mr. Hester, who was himself in fourteen foster homes in seventeen years. According to him, "Parenthood is a privilege, not a right. If you're irresponsible in your privilege, someone else has to do the job. . . ." He believes that a child is placed in foster care because the family has failed, ". . . but if we put a child in number two foster home, then *we've* failed," he says.

Although foster care was designed as a short-term arrangement ending in either adoption or the child's return to a competent parent, it has become a sort of twilight zone for children.

▲ PLANNING FOR SUCCESS

While instances of abuse in foster care homes sometimes make newspaper headlines, many agencies prevent such abuse by closely screening families who apply for fostering. At La Hacienda, potential foster parents go through a three- to six-month licensing process that includes fingerprinting on the state and federal level. The agency interviews both spouses (or the single parent) and any other children in the family. It conducts training programs and a health inspection to be sure that the children are placed in clean and safe homes. Foster parents also undergo physical exams to make sure that their own health is good. But more supervision is needed, say the experts, because situations change. A household that passes inspection for fostering may change and no longer represent a safe home for a child.

One approach to ending the foster care problem is kinship foster care, in which relatives receive foster care stipends for taking in children who would otherwise be in foster care with strangers. Kinship care is one way of increasing the number of minority children who stay within their cultural circle. However, it is not without problems.

Glen Hester reports that children have been killed in kinship homes in New York City. In these cases, the subsidies sound inviting, but the foster parents really aren't prepared to deal with the everyday life of the children, and, as a result, they take out their anger on the kids. He proposes that if "we're going to have a kinship home program, I want them to be under the same standards as a foster home." While some look at kinship homes as a first alternative, Glen Hester looks at them as a last alternative.

The system still needs reforms if permanency for children is the goal. The costs and structure of the existing foster care system offer little incentive to move a child into the adoptive process. One way to help children achieve permanency would be to give foster families more financial support should they choose to adopt when the children's ties with their parents are severed. Currently, all of the reimbursements a family gets through foster care are potentially lost when it adopts the child. Some reimbursements can be gained through adoption subsidies, but usually on a case-by-case basis. This leaves some families who love their foster children and want to keep them unable to adopt because they can't afford to. Instead, they keep the children in long-term foster care, and accept the fact that an adoptive home will have to be found.

Because foster parents are provided with money, and adoptive parents usually are not, some critics say that foster parents are "in it for the money." Ms. Goldsmith of La Hacienda finds that hard to believe because fostering is a full-time job. "Foster parents are very special people," she says. "They love children. They're very dedicated. It's their mission in life to care for children." However, she does acknowledge that problems can occur. Although she believes that most people get into foster care for all the right reasons, she has seen some foster parents *develop* the wrong reasons. As she explains, "Sometimes people take on too many children and then get used to the reimbursements for many children. They then develop a lifestyle—do additions on their homes or whatever—and have to continue to take that many children."

In Nevada, foster homes are only allowed two children unless they are a sibling group. In other states, such as Arizona, the system relies on families that can take in many children at once. And although the need for foster care is growing, the fact that more and more women are working has reduced the number of foster parents.

One group having a positive impact on permanency planning in foster care is Downey Side, with offices located in New York, Massachusetts, and Connecticut. Downey Side attempts to find permanent homes for pre-adolescent and adolescent children as a way of preventing homelessness. If children are discharged from foster care with no place to call home, many of them wind up in prison or in a homeless shelter. "These children are not faring well," writes Pat O'Brien, director of the New York Region Downey Side, "because the child welfare system in our country has not taken it upon itself to help these children develop a lasting relationship in their life when they were in foster care."[2]

According to Mr. O'Brien, adoption, or developing a permanent lasting relationship with at least one adult, is the only hope for our older foster care children. Currently, Downey Side is trying to force those working in the system to accept the responsibility of finding "interdependent living" relationships for its children rather than encouraging "independent living." Today, in some states, at age fourteen foster children can sign a waiver stating that they don't want to be adopted and that they want their goal changed to "independent living." But, claims Mr. O'Brien, at age fourteen they can't vote, drive a car, sign a legally binding contract, and more. How can we believe that they are old enough to choose independent living?

Mr. O'Brien firmly believes that all human beings want to belong somewhere. With that in mind, his goal at Downey Side is to match older foster children with adoptive parents. He believes that despite criticism of his idea, every older foster child is adoptable. His object is to sensitize the public and those within the foster care system so that the latter is obligated to continuously find permanency for every child up to the date of their discharge from the system. Downey Side offers an eight-week "exploring adoption" course for anyone considering the adoption of an older child.

Another agency, Miracle Makers, works hard to help children in foster care look at the positive side of it. As Eddie Lacewell says, he tells foster youngsters, "Find out what you want to do. Don't look at foster care as being your last stop. Let it be your first stop." The organization works to help teenagers establish living skills so that when they are ready to live on their own they can do it successfully.

Many family policy experts believe that the foster care system needs a major overhaul, not just fine tuning. For now, foster care remains controversial because of the many reforms it needs. Yet those dedicated to improving the system remain indebted to the foster parents who work within its boundaries to give loving and safe temporary homes to children growing up in uncertain circumstances.

7 ▲ SPECIAL-NEEDS ADOPTIONS AND UNCONVENTIONAL PARENTS

"Special needs" is a term used to describe the many children who don't find permanent homes easily or at all. These include African Americans and other minorities, those with physical or mental challenges, and any group of siblings who must be adopted together. The term also applies to children who are seen as too old for a market that favors infants.

In most states, special-needs children make up the vast majority of youngsters handled by the public adoption agencies. Yet in any given year, only one third of the approximately 36,000 available special-needs children will find a permanent family. Some of the rest can be found in hospitals as boarder babies, infants who have been left behind at birth by addicted or otherwise incapable mothers. Others live in institutions or group homes and, as mentioned earlier, the majority spend their childhood in foster care. According to a 1990 report by the North American Council on Adoptable Children (NACAC), infants and young children, many with medical complications and physical and mental limitations caused by prenatal drug exposure, make up the fastest growing group of children entering foster care today. This fact has prompted some adoption specialists to call for a return to orphanages and institutional care. However, NACAC considers that to be a "poor response to system failures," and advocates other alternatives, including specialized treatment foster homes.[1]

Children with mental and physical challenges may be the most difficult to place. Yet those in the adoption community firmly believe that there is a home for every child. However, professionals like Janet Dawes from the ACH always investigate the motivation of any couple or single person wanting to adopt a special-needs child. She will ask questions such as, "Have you ever worked with handicapped children before?" "How do you plan to alter the home?" "How will you intervene on that child's behalf?"

According to Lexanne Downey of Catholic Social Services, parents who adopt special-needs children with medical or emotional problems "need to have a total acceptance of the worst outcome. They need to expect the best but be ready for the worst." Her feeling is that it is important for adoptive parents to accept children for who they are and themselves for what they can handle. She also believes that nobody should take a special-needs or minority child because it takes too long to get the child they really want.

Most experts agree that special-needs adoption is not for everyone. Parents who adopt special-needs children speak of the rewards as often as they do the difficulties. Some parents are not able to deal with severely handicapped children. Then again, as Doris Halbich of the Arizona Foster Information Center says, "What one family considers a disability another family does not."

At a time when there is a shortage of couples to adopt the growing number of special-needs children, adoption officials have been forced to consider a broader definition of what constitutes a family. In 1987, a White House task force recommended that states eliminate barriers to adoption by singles, working couples, older people, and the physically handicapped. All of these "unconventional" parents were at one time not considered potential adoptive parents. But times have changed. The number of single parents who adopt increases yearly. Usually infants are denied to them because the birthparents want a couple. However, this is not always the case.

▲ SINGLE ADOPTIVE PARENTS

Kathy, Jesse's birthmother, introduced in chapter 3, went over the files of many potential adoptive couples. Although she wouldn't say the couples had faults, they did write things about themselves that bothered her. For instance, one couple didn't want to meet with the birthmother, so for Kathy they were completely out. Then she came to Teresa's file. Although she wanted a couple to raise her child, and wasn't looking for a single mother, Kathy couldn't help but be impressed with how well Teresa was able to raise three children (two of them adopted) and still hold a full-time teaching position. Furthermore, Kathy thought that Teresa was "very thorough on the application she filled out. She didn't just put one sentence for each question, she put a paragraph. So basically I found out a lot about what type of person she was, and what type of family she had and what she expected if she were to adopt a child and I pretty much had my mind made up. And when I met her that really made my mind set . . . she was the best choice and to be honest, I think that if I looked at ten more files, I would still have picked her."

Twenty years ago, if you had gone to an adoption agency as a single person and applied for a child, you would have been turned down. Some states even had laws forbidding single-parent adoption. Today, with so many biological families splitting up, and more and more households headed by women, the single-parent household is a familiar one, thus eliminating the stigma. Thousands of children in this country and elsewhere in the world are living in the loving permanent adoptive homes provided by single men and women. Perhaps as many as 25 percent of special-needs adoptions are by single parents. In fact, single parents are sometimes preferred for special-needs children because they can give them the focused attention they need, without being distracted by their own relationship problems.

"Sometimes I'm amazed I made this family," reported Lorie Greer, a single adoptive mother in San Francisco.[2] Ms. Greer, a nurse, had always wanted to be a mother and have many children. But by the time she was in her mid-thirties, she still wasn't married and rather than not have children, she chose to look into adopting.

Things started falling into place for her when she saw a story on cable television about the Fragile Infant Special Care program of the San Francisco Department of Social Services. The program was looking for experienced foster parents or trained medical people to care for sick babies at home. Ms. Greer took a ten-week foster parenting course, and underwent all the other formalities to be certified as a foster parent. When she was accepted, she quit her job, accepted the monthly stipend of $1,400 from the county, and soon had a very sick two-month-old infant, Max, in her care. Max was a drug baby, his mother having been on crack.

When Max was six months old, Lorie was asked if she would care for a second baby. He is Miguel, an eight-month-old boy with AIDS. His own mother had died from AIDS three months after he was born. The three have molded into a family.

When Max's social worker called shortly after his first birthday and said that he was well enough to be put up for adoption, Lorie immediately burst into tears. She couldn't bear the thought of giving him up. Lorie must wait, unsure of what will happen to her family. For now, she knows that Miguel will die someday. And Max's mother has not yet relinquished her parental rights. But, day by day, Lorie, Max, and Miguel are a family.

Single people have to think through their decision carefully. Most single parents work full-time and are financially responsible for their families. Although agencies are eager to place children with special needs, applicants who are single must pass many requirements, including that of age. Factors such as being a homeowner, or having a great deal of savings are not as important as stability, maturity, and flexibility. Agencies will want to know the single person's plans for child care, as well as the kind of support network of friends and family he or she can call upon.

However, regardless of the potential problems, single adoptive parents have already had many success stories. The latest research indicates that children raised in adoptive single-parent families score favorably with other adopted children and show a healthy involvement with friends and family as well with others in their age group. It has been shown that it is the instability of broken homes, rather than the absence of a parent, that causes difficulty for a child.[3]

Researchers who conducted an eight-year study of twenty-two single adoptive parents reported that the single parents studied "lead busy lives and seem to manage the demands of jobs, home, and parenting with a sure touch."[4] Although there are certainly more single adoptive women than single adoptive men, more and more men are becoming adoptive parents. In some cases, single men are the placement of choice. This is especially true for boys who have had traumatic histories and need strong male role models and guidance in an accepting, loving environment.

Yet, the controversy over single parents remains, since in the traditional view of parenting the child needs both parents for healthy growth and development. Singles who want to adopt have obstacles from outside the adoption community, too, with family and friends frequently not understanding their decision and trying to dissuade them from it.

Although the governmental task force mentioned earlier opposed adoption by homosexuals, growing numbers of gay men and women—who are generally spurned by ordinary adoption agencies—have sought special-needs children. A homosexual couple on Long Island, New York, have taken in a fragile nineteen-month-old baby infected with the AIDS virus and abandoned by his addict mother at birth. They are also preparing to adopt a two-year-old with AIDS.

The Federal Government has taken a few steps to make special-needs adoption more attractive. In 1980, Congress passed a major reform of adoption and child-welfare laws. Among other things, it offered a federal stipend of $200 to $300 a month to some adoptive parents of special-needs children.

Beyond the studies there are the children, many of whom would love to share their lives with at least one caring person.

RIGHTS OF BIRTHFATHERS

Often, when people talk about unmarried teenage parents, they are referring only to the birthmother. Her partner, whether a teenager himself, or older, may be ignored or labeled the villain in the scenario. He is the "cad" who got the girl "in trouble" and then deserted her, so that she had no choice but to surrender her child for adoption. While it is true that the majority of unwed birthfathers are not involved in the adoption process, this is not always by choice. And, although the prevailing notion is that most single fathers don't care about their unplanned children, Jon Ryan says otherwise. Mr. Ryan runs the National Organization for Birthfathers and Adoption Reform (NO-BAR), a support and advocacy group for birthfathers. According to Mr. Ryan, most single fathers are concerned about the child of an unexpected pregnancy, have a significant relationship with the mother, and want to be involved in what happens to the child.

Sometimes the father may only seem like a cad because he is kept from being involved by the birthmother and/or the agency or lawyer she contacts. In fact, the birthmother may choose not to tell her partner she is pregnant. Perhaps she fears that the birthfather might try to talk her into an option she doesn't want. She may worry that he will insist on her getting an abortion, or on marrying him, when she is unwilling to do either. Or she may fear that he will want custody of the child, although she believes that he would be an unfit parent. Then again, she may decide to conceal her pregnancy for a variety of other reasons, including anger at the birthfather for having deserted her. On a more altruistic note, she may be trying to shield him from a painful emotional situation or one she doesn't think that he can handle.

Exactly how involved birthfathers should be in deciding what to do about an unplanned child remains controversial. While groups like NOBAR believe fathers should have equal rights, others strongly disagree. Some states legislate against it, and some men agree with them. Until the recent development of tests that can accurately prove paternity, birthfathers could easily challenge any accusation of fatherhood. If they chose to turn their backs on the situation, it was often out of the fear that they would be forced to pay child support, or would have to marry the mother even though they did not want to.

Jon Ryan reports that the strong bias against birthfathers by birthmothers and workers in the adoption community is everywhere. He believes that birthfathers are kept out of the adoption process because their input is thought to complicate the process for those who make money from it. He recalls a recent adoption conference at which an adoption lawyer, who practices in a state that requires both birthparents to sign a consent to adopt, told the audience that the way he deals with birthfathers is to send them the consent to sign and return. If they refuse, he tells them that they have two options. They can either sign the paper or look forward to eighteen years of child support, yet no interaction with the child. "To a young man that can be pretty overwhelming," says Mr. Ryan.

In some states, such as California, the father's rights are currently on the same level as those of potential adoptive parents, with courts weighing who could give the child a better home. Often, the adoptive parents, being older and more stable financially, will win the case. This law was recently challenged, and California is now struggling to write a new law.

▲ A MORE POSITIVE PICTURE

But, in all fairness, the picture is not totally bleak. Some adoption agencies claim to welcome the opportunity to involve birthfathers in the adoption process. Janet Dawes of the ACH says that she wishes more birthfathers would stand by the birthmothers and not just walk away from the situation. According to Ms. Dawes, counselors at ACH are open to working with both partners in an unintended pregnancy. And Mr. Ryan says that his studies indicate that when birthfathers are allowed to get involved in making adoption decisions, they become sympathetic to the birthmother's anguish and continue their support even after the child has been adopted.[1]

NOBAR is helping unmarried birthfathers become more knowledgeable about their options, as well as more vocal about their right to have an equal say in what happens to their child. And, in a mounting number of cases, single birthfathers are electing to raise their children rather than give them up for adoption, even if the relationship with the birthmother is over. The time is ripe for upgrading the rights of fathers; there are now 1.6 million homes headed by single fathers. Most of these single fathers are divorced, but a significant number have not been married. In fact, many federal court decisions and changes in adoption laws during the past twenty years have expanded the rights of unwed fathers to have a say in their children's future.

Until the early 1970s, unwed fathers had no legal rights to their children. An unmarried father's permission was not required if a mother wished to release the baby for adoption, while the mother could stop an adoption by simply withholding consent. The law began to change in 1972 with the landmark Supreme Court decision in the case of *Stanley* v. *Illinois*. It recognized for the first time that birthfathers have a legal claim to their children.[2] The decision made it unconstitutional to not notify fathers of proceedings to terminate their parental rights.

Today, in many states, the father's signature—provided he can be found—is almost always required before an adoption can be finalized. If the father is missing, and efforts to find him prove fruitless, the court is petitioned to sever his rights. After a certain period of time, the child can be released for adoption. In many states, an unwed father is permitted to deny consent to an adoption only if he openly declares himself the father, offers financial support for the child, and has lived with the child or its mother for a designated period of time.

▲ STATE LAWS NEED IMPROVEMENT

But state laws are often far from adequate, according to fathers' rights advocates, and even good laws can be circumvented. In Texas, a father who has not legally married the mother of their child does not fit the state's legal definition of a parent. Therefore, he has no legal say in a child's availability for adoption. In some cases, pregnant women from other states with more liberal laws have flown to Texas, where their plane fare was provided by a well-known maternity home. Then, before the father could figure out what had happened, the woman had her baby and gave it up for adoption. In such cases, the father has no idea where to even start fighting to get his child back.

In pre-1972 Illinois, state law expressly said that "an unwed father and his child may never visit one another."[3] Today, for a father in Illinois, and many other states, to intervene in adoption proceedings, he has to have lived with his child for at least half the child's life before the adoption takes place.

Arizona, by contrast, is a state with a relatively good law for birthfathers. It gives them broad rights in adoptions, requiring the consent of both birthparents to adopt. However, as Shawn Cunningham knows, there are loopholes in the law. In 1989, Shawn found out that his girlfriend was pregnant. Both were eighteen at the time. The girlfriend, who already had a two-year-old daughter, did not want to keep the child. Shawn wanted custody of the baby. He helped deliver Amber on July 10, 1989, and for two days held her, helped care for her, and gave emotional support to his girlfriend. He never signed a consent to adopt, but when he was leaving the hospital, with Amber in his arms, his girlfriend asked to hold the baby. When he gave Amber to her, she in turn gave the baby to a wealthy prospective adoptive couple who fled with the newborn to their home in California.

Thus began two years of Shawn trying to get Amber back through California courts, and the adoptive parents trying to prove that Shawn was an unfit parent. He won six court hearings in California, only to have the court system send the case back to Tucson, where the adoptive parents now have temporary guardianship while the court proceedings continue. Shawn estimates that the case has cost him $150,000 so far and, needless to say, the emotional toll has been high.

As far as Shawn can see, the laws are being manipulated. Through an intermediary (Shawn could not speak to the media, since his case is still pending) Shawn advised any birthfather involved in a similar situation to stand his ground, find out his legal rights, do everything legally, and from the beginning establish his parental rights and keep track of all his expenses in relation to the child and mother.

Meanwhile, other states, including California and New York, are currently rewriting their laws to give birthfathers greater rights. In 1990, in a unanimous decision, the New York State Court of Appeals granted the right to veto an adoption to fathers who have shown an interest in their children and a willingness to assume custody. The law applies only to adoption cases involving children younger than six months. State law requires that a child older than six months have an unwed father's consent if he has maintained "substantial and continuous" contact with the child. Some experts in family law consider the new law "an opportunity for chaos" because the courts will have to decide the appropriate criteria for determining whether the father has shown interest.[4]

▲ LOOKING TOWARD A BETTER FUTURE

With state laws changing and birthfathers becoming more organized and adamant in their demands for equal rights, it appears that whether or not their partners support their involvement, it is imperative that birthmothers be honest and tell them about their proposed adoption plans. Keeping their pregnancy a secret is usually discouraged, since secrecy can backfire, with the father disrupting the child's adoption when he demands his rights. Agencies generally advise women to clear the situation with the birthfather beforehand rather than risk legal and emotional problems later on.

There is another issue to address: Many adoption specialists feel very strongly that children have a need and a right to know their personal history. This is critical knowledge in their developmental process, as we shall explore in more detail in the next chapter. This is also information that calls for an adoptee to know his or her birthfather, or certainly to know about him.

For today, and for many years to come, the issue of fathers' rights promises to remain a controversial one in legal circles. With laws so easily circumvented, even in model states, unwed fathers still do not enjoy the same legal protection as unwed mothers. And, while NOBAR continues to work for reform at the state level, at present its major concentration is on efforts to influence a national panel that is putting together a comprehensive adoption act intended to standardize adoption laws in every state. Jon Ryan and other advocates of fathers' rights want to make sure that birthfathers' interests are served if and when the act is drafted and put into effect.

SEARCHES

"Now I feel complete and I know it's okay to be me."

"I feel that a hole was filled that I didn't know was there."

"I feel connected for the first time. Now I can put this behind me and get on with my life."

"Even though I respect the fact that my birthmom was promised confidentiality, I feel that I have a right to know."

—Voices of some adoptees who have chosen
to search for their birthparents

In the past, adoption agencies used to recommend that adoptive parents tell their children certain stories as they grew up. Adoptees loved to hear these stories, which were much like fairy tales. In them, the adoptive parents wanted a little child and they went to the nursery to look for one. They walked up and down the aisles, looking at all the little babies and when they came to their son or daughter, they said, "That's the one we want, that one's perfect for us." And that's how the child came to be part of their family.

In reality, life is not like a fairy tale. And while adoption stories may sound charming, they don't diminish the desire of many children to know their roots, to find out in whose body they developed. At the same time, adoption agencies would tell the birthparents to forget about the child. As one birthfather recalls, "I remember a social worker said, 'Someday you'll forget.' But you don't forget. How the heck can you forget the birth of a child?"

Eventually, many parents who cannot forget, and many adoptees who want to know the truth, begin to search for the missing part of their life story. But the very idea of searching is controversial. Many people question whether the children of closed adoptions should have the right to search for their birthparents or whether birthparents should be allowed to seek out their natural children years after they have placed them for adoption. Your feelings on the issue puts you on one side or the other of another highly charged adoption debate, that of privacy versus the right to know.

▲ THE SEARCH FOR IDENTITY

Searches are the very stuff of romance novels and soap operas. They are mysteries to unravel, with no guarantee of how they will turn out. Those who support the right to search say that non-adoptees take for granted biological roots that the children of closed adoptions are barred from. Whether biological children are content with their families or not, they have the security of knowing who they look like and who their ancestors were. The past is not hidden from them in sealed files. Adoptees who have found their parents after searching often speak of a lifelong emptiness that wasn't filled until they found the missing link, the person who gave birth to them. Initial searches are almost always for the birthmother. Interest in finding the birthfather comes later.

Adoptees may need to know their medical history so they can anticipate possible hereditary diseases or conditions. But the motivation most often mentioned for searching is a need to connect with one's beginnings, to know who they got their chin or eyes from, to come face-to-face with their own ancestry. Says Kay Gartrell, president of Triad, a search group in Tucson, Arizona, "We're not trying to find parents, we're trying to find identity." Adoptees feel alienated from others, even from themselves when they lack knowledge of their biological origin. They also feel a need to understand their genetically influenced behavior, the roots of their interests and talents, and why they act and react the way they do.

Even though children may dearly love their adoptive parents, it is often natural for them to want to know all they can about their own personal history. At a recent Triad meeting, an adoptee who is presently searching said that adoptees often don't ask questions because they don't want to hurt their adoptive parents. But their silence doesn't mean that the questions aren't there. "If they [adoptees] don't ask, they're suppressing the questions," she said. "I would ask them how they feel and try to remember that love can be boundless and not tied into two parents." She had personally wanted to ask her adoptive parents many questions, but held back so as not to seem disloyal. Now that both her parents have died, she is searching.

People often become more intense about searching for their biological origins when they reach adolescence, a time in which children struggle to clarify their own identity. It is then that some begin to feel driven to end their biological anonymity.

As the number of searchers grows, more and more adult adoptees are petitioning the law to give them the same rights and privileges other citizens take for granted.

They argue that searches conducted by responsible citizens should not be feared, ignored, or prolonged due to legal roadblocks. One adoptee, who had the consent of both her adoptive parents and her birthparents to see her own original birth certificate, nevertheless had that right denied her by the court.

However, not all adoptees want to search. Some have no desire to seek out their birthparents. This may be due to respect for their adoptive parents, fear of learning the truth, or because they simply do not care. Whether they are suppressing their true feelings or not remains a subject of debate.

Critics of searches say that they break legal contracts, which should be the cornerstone of adoption. They argue that everyone should respect confidentiality when it is requested. Furthermore, searches can disrupt many lives, and can open up a can of worms for everyone involved. Just because one side wants to locate the other doesn't mean the object of the search wants to be found. The worst scenario is for adoptees to be turned down and experience a second rejection from their birthparents. Perhaps the birthparents have made new lives for themselves and prefer to forget the existence of a child they relinquished. The birthparents may have a whole family that is unaware of the adoptee's existence. Then, too, searches may reveal dark secrets and bring about unforeseen heartbreak.

Arguing on the flip side are those who insist that it is always best to know the truth, regardless of what it may be. If not, a big gap will always exist. Besides, the search may end on a happy note, with birthparents welcoming the birth child and eager to learn about the full-grown person they had to give up long ago. A successful search also gives birthparents the opportunity to explain why they did what they did. Time and again searches prove worthwhile. In a letter to the editor in the *New York Times*, Barbara Cohen, New Jersey Coordinator for ALARM (Advocating

Legislation for Adoption Reform Movement), wrote, "I am an adoptee, who through a very arduous, emotional, and expensive search found my birth family. As a result of knowing the truth, I have found a sense of completeness and wholeness that I never thought possible."

According to some specialists, even a search without a happy ending can be fruitful, since it provides a valuable psychological function, allowing seekers to have control over forces over which they previously did not.[1]

Because searches affect everyone involved in the adoption triad, the needs and concerns of all parties should be addressed. Perhaps that is why in many cases adoptees do not begin to search until their adoptive parents have died. Other searches are triggered by significant events in the searcher's life, such as a marriage, the birth of a child, the illness of a child, or their own illness.

While the privacy versus the right to know debate continues, more and more adoptees are searching. According to the American Adoption Congress (AAC) in New York City, more than 60,000 Americans are engaged in searches for their birthparents, or for the children they relinquished at birth. Today, females make up the majority of search group members, although an increasing number of men are joining as our society becomes more accepting of men expressing their emotional needs. There are over 500 support groups for searchers in the United States and Canada.

▲ REGISTRIES, NATIONAL ORGANIZATIONS, AND LOCAL GROUPS

Currently, the AAC and ALMA (Adoptees Liberty Movement Association) are lobbying to change state laws that protect the confidentiality of adoption records. Today, mutual consent registries exist in twenty-two states. These registries match adoptees and birthparents who are looking for each other. This method prevents forced reunions.

Birthparents who want to maintain their privacy can do so, and adoptees can be ensured that the person they seek wants to be contacted.

One of the most successful registries is the International Soundex Reunion Registry in Carson City, Nevada, a private, nonprofit center that since 1975 has matched more than 2,200 people. Interested parties fill out an application by mail which stays on file and is deemed legal consent for contact between the two parties of a match. When a match occurs, the registrar makes a person-to-person phone call to notify them. Neither the identity of the birthparents nor the adopted child is revealed unless both parties want a reunion.

Searchers usually begin by getting involved with a local search group, like Triad in Tucson. Its members meet twice a month to give each other support, exchange search information, and tell their stories. When searches prove fruitful, they share the results of their first contact. Later, they may bring in photographs from their reunion to pass around. The stories run the gamut from those with happy endings to those with sad finales, from searches that took a few months to others that have been going on for several years.

At a recent meeting, a birthmother who had tracked down and phoned her twenty-year-old birthdaughter, was trying to come to terms with the fact that the daughter did not want to meet her yet. "Wait until she has children of her own," advised Valerie King, another Triad member, an adoptee who had recently had her first reunion with her birthparents. Ms. King, a mother in her late twenties, had brought along snapshots of her reunion with her birthparents, who had married two years after relinquishing her, and then went on to have three more children. Valerie called her birthparents by their first names and talked about how her sister was cold to her, her birthmother eager to protect the sister, and her birthfather the most delighted of them all to have her back in their lives again.

Others at the meeting exchanged tips about where to go for birth records, which woman in what government office liked to help searchers find their records, how to sign up with the various registries, and how to get information from the agency they had originally been placed with. Newcomers to the meeting were made aware that changes in Arizona state laws now permit the agencies to unite birthparents and adoptees if that is what both desire. Where adoption is more closed, adoptees can receive "nonidentifying information" from agencies; this refers to general facts about the birthparents without revealing names and addresses. It may include the circumstances under which they gave up the child, their ages, hobbies, interests, occupations, ethnic heritage, and medical backgrounds.

Then, armed with all the nonidentifying information they can obtain, searchers and their advisers begin their detective work. Searches may include visits and calls to doctors' offices, religious facilities, family service agencies, homes for unwed mothers, funeral homes, hospitals, schools, government offices, and libraries. Adoptees may have to scrutinize school yearbooks; city directories; divorce, annulment, and inheritance records; death certificates; legal petitions to adopt; phone directories; Social Security records; and more. They are likely to encounter many false leads, and experience many highs and lows. Some searches take many years, with the biggest obstacles being sealed records, which may by law only be opened by court order if good cause can be shown. However, advocates usually don't advise the legal route because the courts are reluctant to open records, and strong medical reasons are usually the only exceptions to the rule. Other searches may be over in just a matter of days or even hours. Success is partly due to luck, but mostly due to imagination and patience. Being a bit obsessive doesn't hurt either.

One person to recently search for her child is Laura Watkins Lewis, a writer who had given up her infant son when she was seventeen, having been led to believe that he would be happier if she were no longer a part of his life. In an article in the *Washington Post*,[2] she recalled being told that she would get over the hurt and have other children to replace him. She found that not to be true. She did marry and have more children, but she never forgot her first son. She thought of him most often on his birthday and on Mother's Day. When he was a teenager, she finally decided that she had to search, had to find out how he was, had to help him understand why she had given him up.

She wanted him to know that she had become pregnant in the tenth grade, and was counseled by her caseworker that adoption was the selfless, mature, and responsible thing to do. In looking back, she realized that she had not been informed of any rights she might have had as a birthmother, any alternatives, or that there might be risks involved for her and her child. Instead, she was asked to choose between her child growing up in poverty with her, or growing up with a well-rounded family that would give her child a better life than she could. She had to make a list comparing what she could offer her son with what his idealized adoptive parents could. She remembers that all she could put down on her list was love.

When the agency social worker took her son away, she was told that he was going directly to a loving professional couple. Later she discovered that he was in foster care for three months. "If he had been unwanted and ended up in foster care or an institution for the rest of his life, I would never have known. I had unknowingly signed away my right to be informed." She remembers feeling a protective numbing after the adoption that kept her from crying about her son once he was taken away from her; she considers it a feminine equivalent of combat shock.

Many years later, and determined to find him, she contacted the adoption agency, where a social worker told her that they knew nothing about her son and were not allowed to reveal anything if they did. Before she gave up her search, a social worker referred her to Concerned United Birthparents (CUB), a national advocacy organization made up primarily of women who had given up their babies for adoption. CUB helps birthmothers search, in what sometimes turns out to be an expensive process, for their relinquished children although, "Some people think CUB is neurotic and self-flagellating, that it encourages the opening of old wounds, fosters wallowing in 'irretrievable disaster,' makes women dramatize what they would better forget."[3] But for many searchers, CUB is a blessing.

Ms. Lewis attended CUB meetings and heard many stories. Some had happy endings, like the story in which the adoptive family invited the birthmother to join them for Thanksgiving. Other searchers were rejected by their children and/or by their children's adoptive parents. Several were threatened with legal action just for writing to ask about their children. Some discovered that their children did not know they were adopted. Others found their children but chose not to make contact until their children sought them out.

Eventually, with advice from a search expert and support from other birthmothers, the writer found her son. He was contacted by his birthfather, who sent him a letter, along with three business cards: his, the birthmother's husband's, and that of an attorney who would act as intermediary if the boy wanted information. The decision was left up to him.

He called her a month later and admitted that he had never wondered about her. But now he was ready to meet her and his birthfather. They got together that weekend at the same marina where his birthmother and birthfather had first met twenty years before.

There, they sat on a sun deck talking and showing

photographs. The mother could see reflections of other family members in his gestures, his features, and his expressions. For this search, the ending was worthwhile, the need to know and be given a chance to explain was satisfied.

▲ OTHER SEARCHES

Another searcher is Carl, a member of Triad. In a film made by Triad he told how he relinquished the daughter his girlfriend had when she was seventeen and he was nineteen. He believes that the outside pressure from both their parents made them believe they were doing the right thing. Now he thinks that it was more a matter of their parents wanting to bury the predicament as soon as possible, before relatives and neighbors found out about it, than a decision made in the best interests of the child and birthparents. He can still remember seeing his birthdaughter in the hospital for the first time, and talking with the birthmother about whose eyes the baby had, whose nose. Many years later, birthfather and child were reunited, meeting at a restaurant where they sat for two hours, showing pictures and explaining their lives to each other. "This must be what heaven is like . . . ." said Carl. "Since I've met her, I feel like I've been reborn. I feel more at peace . . . it's a good feeling to know that life's been good to her and that she's okay. But the question I still have is did I do the right thing letting her go?"

Another Triad member whose search was successful reported, "After I found my daughter, I wrote her parents for permission. They gave the letter to her. I got a thirteen-page letter in the mail. The reunion was wonderful. She flew out here for Thanksgiving. For the first time, I could touch her. We spent six glorious days getting to know each other . . . for the first time, I had all of my children under the same roof together. It had been a hole and now it's filled with love. I've grown, I've become a complete person."

Search advisers generally warn searchers against barging in on and shocking their biological children or birthparents. An initial contact by phone or through the mail is recommended to give the object of the search time to consider what may turn out to be a highly emotional meeting. As Joe Soll of the American Adoption Congress in New York says, it takes time to build up a history of trust. But, very often, once trust is established, the birth relative can become a friend of the adoptee.[4]

When birthparents are found, it can end years of fantasizing. "The truth is always better than not knowing," says one adoptee, "even if my mother isn't Marilyn Monroe, as I had imagined she was." The people involved go on to discover similarities; they may walk the same, sleep the same, or have the same taste in food, clothes, or cars. It is a relief, say searchers, to realize where their curly hair and clear skin came from in a family that had straight hair and freckles, or where their musical talent came from in a family that was by and large tone deaf.

Yet the debate about searching continues. In a letter to the editor in the *New York Times,* Dr. David H. Wisotsky wrote, "As a pediatrician and adoptive parent, I have found that, where adoption is discussed openly, honestly, and gently, the need to search doesn't necessarily exist, contrary to the outcry of the vocal minority of adult adoptees who feel that records should be opened unconditionally."[5] Minority or not, searchers appear to be growing in number, and the poignancy of searches continues to make the news.

A recent *Time Magazine* article covered the search of Patricia Szymczak, a reporter with the *Chicago Tribune,* who at age thirty-six decided to pursue the quest "she had contemplated since childhood: finding her biological mother." Adopted in infancy, she began her search with her birthmother's name and hometown, which she had gotten from her adoptive mother when she turned eighteen. "The long search ended with a three-hour call. By the end of the conversation, it was after midnight on the second Sunday in May. Patricia Szymczak smiled and wished her newfound relation a happy Mother's Day."[6]

10 ARE ADOPTEES DIFFERENT?

"Eddy was watching Sesame Street and he said to me, 'I came out of your tummy, didn't I?' I realized that some actress on the show was explaining about being pregnant. And there it was, the question I'd been dreading. I'd been told that he would ask it someday, that they all do, but first of all, I couldn't believe he really was asking it, and second of all, I wasn't prepared for the way it made me feel. Like, it brought back all those feelings I had when I was going to the doctor, trying to become pregnant. All my . . . frustration and anger and sense of loss. And, there was Eddy, waiting for an answer. I said to him, 'No, you didn't come out of my tummy.'

"I could see that I had really confused him. The poor kid had looked so sure of himself a minute ago. And before I had a chance to think about what to say next, he asked me, 'Then whose tummy did I come out of?'

"I told him, 'You came from the tummy of a very nice lady.' So then he said, 'I know who she was. It was Mary, right?' Mary's his babysitter. 'No,' I said, 'it wasn't Mary.' Eddy looked kind of puzzled then. But a second later he was grinning, like he finally got it, he had finally put the pieces of the puzzle together. 'Then it was Rachel, wasn't it?' he asked. Rachel's our social worker.

" 'No,' I said, 'but she was very nice and she loves you very much.' Then Eddy got distracted by something else on TV and I felt like, you know, saved by the bell. But I'm sure it will come up again. I only hope I handle it better next time."

—Susan S., an adoptive mother

"I'll never forget how I found out the truth. I was in my teens and my best friend, Beth, and I were getting ready for a surprise birthday party for my mother. And Beth made some remark about another friend's not being told something and how that was so different from, as she put it, 'you always knowing you're adopted.'

"At first her words didn't register. 'What did you say?' I asked.

" 'You know, it's not like you always knowing that you're adopted,' Beth replied.

" 'I'm adopted?' I asked. By then I was in shock. The idea had never entered my mind.

" 'Oh, you mean you don't know?' Beth asked, and then she kept on apologizing for having told me. I remember going through the whole party in shock. Years later, when I got pregnant, even though I knew things wouldn't work out with the father, I couldn't give up my child. But if I did, it would have had to be an open adoption, not a closed adoption like I had. I wouldn't want anyone to go through what I've gone through. It's so weird to not know my birthmother or whether I've got any biological brothers or sisters floating around out there."

—Julie L., an adoptee

"I'll never forget this: I was ten years old and with my adoptive family for a month at the most when we got this assignment in school to do a family tree. And here I was, having been in seven foster homes before I got adopted. I felt like crawling under a rock! It was horrible. But then I talked to Mom and she came through for me. I decided it was okay to use Mom and Dad's family tree because at least they knew their own backgrounds. But . . . teachers can be so insensitive sometimes."

—John S., adoptee

"Being adopted never meant very much to me one way or the other. It was just something we were, but Mom and Dad have always been there for me and I never thought twice about being different because I was adopted."

—Rita W., adoptee

Do the 1 or 2 percent of all children who are adopted deal with the world differently than biological children? Do they think differently? Do they act differently? Does the world treat them differently?

▲ THE ADOPTED CHILD SYNDROME

The adoption community is divided by the acceptance or rejection of a concept known as the "adopted child syndrome." The belief in such a syndrome is based on the fact that the numbers of adopted children who have trouble at home, at school, and with the law seem to be higher than the numbers among children raised by their biological parents. Those who accept the syndrome say that most adoptees, when compared with non-adoptees, have a slightly higher number of those in need of mental health facilities, and are slightly more often identified in school systems as having neurological or emotional problems.

Studies by Dr. Kent Ravenscroft, of the Georgetown University School of Medicine, are cited as showing that adoptees exhibit aggression more often than non-adoptees, have greater feelings of rootlessness and low-self esteem, and have more learning problems. They are more likely to be depressed, to lie, to steal, to run away, and to have trouble concentrating, according to Dr. Ravenscroft.[1]

Those who reject the adopted child syndrome believe that the studies on which it is based rarely distinguish between children adopted as infants and those adopted later in life. Children adopted when they are older are more likely to suffer from trauma caused by child abuse or from living in one or more unsatisfactory foster homes before their adoption.

Some experts also claim that the numbers may be higher because adoptive parents may more readily seek professional help when they have a family problem than others in society. One reason for this phenomenon is that they already have on-going experience with doctors, having consulted them for many years for an infertility problem. They may also personally know a social worker whom they can ask for help because of having gone through the adoption process.

Some experts also suggest that there can be other good reasons for the existence of special problems. One risk factor can be traced to poor prenatal conditions. The birthmother may have been a teenager who received inadequate care, used drugs or alcohol when pregnant, or had a complicated delivery. These situations could cause long-term problems for the child. Finally, Dr. David Brodzinsky, a psychologist at Rutgers University in New Jersey, believes that the cause of problems for adoptees can be traced to the adoption experience itself.

▲ DR. BRODZINSKY'S STUDY

Dr. Brodzinsky has conducted one of this country's largest studies of adopted children. Funded by the National Institute of Mental Health and other groups, he and his colleagues have studied the development of 130 adopted children. Each adoptee was matched with a non-adoptee of the same age, sex, and family background and structure. The researchers found that until the age of five or six, adoptees and non-adoptees were very similar psychologically. As preschoolers, adoptees are generally content with their parents' explanation of how they were chosen from all the other children in the nursery. But as they grow older and become more logical thinkers, they begin to realize that in order for someone to have chosen them, someone else had to give them up.

Between the ages of eight and eleven adoptees become more able to grasp the meaning of adoption, reports Dr. Brodzinsky. They reflect on the alternatives to relinquishment that the birthparents might have taken. They may feel anger and resentment toward their birthparents as well as fear of rejection by their adoptive parents. At first, claims Dr. Brodzinsky, this experience of loss causes the natural reaction of grief. Natural though it may be, the grieving can trigger temporary behavioral problems, which can result in slightly higher levels of problems at home, at school, and in the community.[2]

During adolescence, the grieving will often become more intense and also more abstract. According to Brodzinsky and his co-researchers, adolescents not only grieve over the loss of the unknown birthparents—which is found among elementary school children as well—but they also grieve for the loss of part of themselves.[3]

But the grief is only part of their problem at this time, since adolescence in general is a period when young people seek a stable sense of who they are. Adopted youngsters may find this task harder than others because they often lack the necessary past history to begin to develop a stable sense of identity.[4]

Yet despite having a slightly greater risk factor for emotional problems than other youngsters, adopted children as a group do well in life, says Brodzinsky. The main point is that they have problems and feelings that are unique to adoptees.

Clinical social worker Priscilla Misner has been asked by many worried birthparents if giving up a child will hurt that child. "I think that's a really important question to ask," says Misner. "You need to know if it damages children for life to be given up for adoption, and I don't think so. Millions of adopted children grow up healthy and wonderful and don't have any big issues. But I think that eventually they all have to deal with facts that others don't have to deal with."

Part of the problem is other children, who may tease adoptees about adoption because they do not understand it. Adoptive parents may contribute to the problem when they try to minimize the significance of being adopted. The parents may try to deny that any difference exists between them and biological families, yet their adopted children very strongly feel a difference. Many adoption experts advise families with adoptees to accept that they are different from biological families. Not better or worse, just different.

Counselors also often advise adoptive parents to avoid secrecy about their child's adoption. "There is something about being someone's dirty secret that is so harmful to children . . . " says Misner. Her feelings stem from both professional and personal interests, since her own husband

106

is an adoptee who felt the burden of being a "secret" on both his adoptive parents and his birthmother.

Like other counselors who support open adoptions, Misner believes that in order to help adoptees develop a mature concept of the meaning of adoption, adoptive parents should begin talking with them about it at an early age, always giving them only as much information as they can handle.

▲ BONDING AND ATTACHMENT PROBLEMS

In her counseling practice, Misner has seen many "bonding and attachment" disorders. "Traditionally, bonding is what they [experts] feel takes place when the baby is still in the womb, and attachment is the process that takes place after birth that strengthens that bond. The major task in the first year of life is to bond . . . babies need to fall in love with their mothers." This process takes place because babies are so dependent on their caretakers. When their needs are met with a lot of love, the babies automatically begin to trust and love in return. According to Misner, this love and desire to be with their parents is the cornerstone of the relationship.

But in talking about adopted children, explains Misner, often that first year doesn't go very well and sometimes children have several different placements before they are placed in an adoptive home. Therefore, they don't have a consistent person to attach to, and the process of attachment might be delayed for them. Misner has worked with a number of children who, by six months old, when they go into an adoptive home, are already showing signs of distress. These may include such extremes as not making eye contact and having a hollow, faraway look.

To help these children, says Misner, you have to start from scratch and work to "put in there what's never been there." She teaches adoptive parents to help children make eye contact and be comfortable doing so, as well as what to look for and what to do so they can help the children to connect right away.

"I've come to understand how critical those early years are. If tiny kids don't get what they need, that is going to have lifelong effects," says Misner. She believes that if a parent is going to relinquish a child for adoption, then for the child's sake it is best the relinquishment be done as soon as possible. She also feels that birthparents should be taught about child development so that they understand how critical the first two years of life are. She believes that it is crucial for parents to help their children love and be loved "and whatever it takes to make that happen is what is best for them."

More and more counselors are coming to believe that an adoptee's life is made easier through an open or semi-open adoption, provided that all parties involved can handle one. This emphasis has in part been strengthened by the 1979 Minnesota Study of Twins Reared Apart, directed by Thomas J. Bouchard. Bouchard studied twins who had been separated at birth, most often because each twin was adopted by a different family. When the researchers brought together 154 members of 77 twin pairs, almost all of whom had not seen each other since infancy, they found the similarities in about half the subjects adopted by different families to be uncanny. Because the study strongly suggests that genes influence human behavior and personality as much as do environmental factors, it gave a boost to those who believe adoptees and adoptive parents should know about the birthparents whose genes the adoptee has inherited.[5]

On an emotional level, open adoption may help adoptees come to terms with who they are. Brodzinsky unequivocably believes that opening records "simply should be done."[6] While this can help children come to terms with their identity, Brodzinsky is aware that how the practice actually affects the children involved is not fully known yet. Researchers have not yet been able to follow the children of open adoption in sizable numbers over a long period of time, and for that reason he approaches openness with caution.

▲ COUNSELING TRENDS

Misner has seen many children wonder about their birthparents. "If they don't have pictures, they wonder what they look like. As they get older they wonder why they gave them up." Ms. Misner helps children put together books about their life which include all the pictures they have and answers to questions they know. Children have many common questions, such as "What was I like as a baby, why couldn't my birthmother take care of me, why did she have so many problems, what is she doing now, is she okay, will I ever see her?" If the children are told that the birthmother has problems, they may worry that she's okay. Others who have not heard from their birthmothers worry that they are going to be kidnapped by them or that a birthmother is some kind of witch, as is sometimes depicted in television programs.

"I think that we would be missing something if we didn't at least check out open adoption. When kids are adopted, we don't pay attention to the whole range of feelings that will bring on and I think that is the beauty of open adoption. It's out in the open. There are no secrets. It's just really up front with the decisions that were made, and the birthparent is continuously giving permission for that child to live with another family and I think that's very positive."

Misner has group sessions for adopted children to help them deal with their own thoughts as well as with the rest of the world. For instance, they may explore how to react if they don't look like the people who adopted them and they get asked, "Is that your mother?" Do they say they're adopted, or explain it, or say, "It's none of your business?" She has done many sessions about being teased and put down because "the general population does not understand adoption. Most kids don't know much about it except it makes someone different."

Today the trend is toward telling children about their adoption; the question is not if they will be told, but when and how to do so. Many believe that you tell adoptees about their adoption from the time they are tiny, and read them stories about it so they understand that another lady gave birth to them, but wasn't able to care for them. By telling the children early, there is no risk of losing their trust when they find out later. It is also important to present the birthmothers in a positive light so the children never feel bad about them or about themselves.

Perhaps one of the hardest things to tell a child is that his or her birth was the result of a rape. At many agencies, potential adoptive parents are asked to indicate what situations and conditions they are open to, ranging from twins and birth defects to social factors, such as dealing with the child of a rape. Those who feel they can parent a child conceived as the result of a rape are given counseling to help them help the child separate the act from the person. Lexanne Downey believes that, "You can honestly say, 'We don't know who your father is but he must have been handsome, because you are.' " She also encourages adoptive parents to help children understand that a parent who committed a rape may have had problems because his own upbringing was difficult.

Misner tries very hard to get birthparents to gather pictures together and have something in writing so that the children have all the information they need to understand why such a big decision was made about them. The key is that it had nothing to do with whether or not they were good, because until children are much older they automatically assume that it was because of them. So adopted children removed from their homes frequently believe it was because of something they did. "I often spend a lot of time talking to them about what babies do normally—they normally cry and poop and that's not bad. It's the grown-ups' job to take care of them and for some reason, whether we know it or not, the parent was not able to do that, or their parents knew ahead of time they would not be able to take care of the baby the way a baby needs to be taken care of, so they decided to let someone else do that."

▲ THE GOOD-BYE SESSION

Whenever possible, if the children are old enough for one, Misner holds a "good-bye session." She held one recently for a birthmother who herself had grown up in a foster home. The children are three and five. They had been living in a foster home, where the foster parents hoped to become their adoptive parents, for one and a half years, and the birthmother decided that she would never be able to take care of them. She also recognized that they loved their foster family. As Ms. Misner says, "I asked her, 'Would you be willing to meet these people and talk to the kids and say good-bye and give them permission to grow up in another family?' And she did. We had lots of tissues, and the adoptive family brought their video camera because, bless their hearts, they recognize it's going to be an ongoing issue and the more material they have to help their kids, the better off their children will be. The birthmom walked them out to their car, and the kids hopped in with this family and she waved good-bye and said 'I love you' and that she was moving to Alaska, so she wouldn't be able to see them. And now she writes to me and calls to ask how they're doing. It doesn't always happen that way."

SURROGATE MOTHERING

Surrogate parenting is a way for couples to have a baby with the help of a third party, a woman who carries the baby for the couple. This third party is known as the surrogate mother. In gestational surrogacy, the couple's full genetic material—the sperm and the egg—are united in the laboratory, then surgically inserted into the surrogate, who carries the baby to term for the couple. In a second type of surrogacy, the surrogate becomes pregnant through artificial insemination with the man's sperm, so that the baby carries one half its genetic material from the father, and one half from the surrogate mother. She carries a child with the intent to relinquish that child to the biological father (the sperm donor), whose wife then adopts the baby. Surrogacy differs from adoption because the couple has a genetic link to the child. As you may imagine, although surrogacy is relatively new, it has already created great waves of controversy around the globe.

Those who oppose it claim it is creating an exploited "breeder class of poor women, renting their wombs to the rich."[1] According to the Coalition Against Surrogacy, the surrogate's contract usually promises her $10,000 upon the delivery of a healthy baby, or $1,000 if the child is stillborn. "This is babyselling pure and simple," states the Coalition's Surrogacy Fact Sheet. Meanwhile, supporters of surrogacy call it a viable alternative to adoption that allows people—if they can afford it—a genetic link for the entire family.

When the average person thinks of surrogacy, he or she generally thinks about its problems, because surrogacy only makes the headlines when something goes wrong. Yet surrogate parenting centers in the United States claim that surrogacy runs smoothly more than 98 percent of the time. And when it does not work, and the surrogate refuses to give up the child, she reportedly was not screened thoroughly enough.

▲ SURROGACY CASES MAKE HEADLINES

Perhaps the surrogacy case that has so far received the most national attention involved a young married woman named Mary Beth Whitehead who contracted for a fee to bear a child for a couple from New Jersey. When Mrs. Whitehead gave birth, she found she could not bear to relinquish the baby girl. Instead of honoring the contract, Mrs. Whitehead and her husband took the infant and fled the state.

The court case that followed centered on who should raise "Baby M," as the news media came to call this very special child. Should the baby go to Mary Beth Whitehead because she delivered her, or to the man whose sperm had helped to create her and who had a contract stipulating that the baby was to be his and his wife's? In the end, the court ruled that living with her biological father, and being visited by her surrogate mother, was in the best interests of Baby M. Since that case in 1988, New Jersey has declared surrogate parenting illegal in that state.

Several other states have done the same, including Arizona, Florida, Michigan, and Washington. Surrogacy is also illegal in certain countries, such as Great Britain, Is-

113

rael, Germany, and Sweden. In France, where it was recently declared illegal, the highest court stated that surrogacy violates a woman's body and improperly undermines the practice of adoption.

California, a state that allows surrogacy, was the site of a recent surrogacy battle. Anna Johnson, a single mother of Native American, white, and African-American ancestry, agreed to bear a surrogate child who would have the sperm of Mark Calvert and the egg of his wife. Mark Calvert is white. His wife, Crispina, who is Filipino, could not carry the child herself because of medical reasons. The Calverts gave Ms. Johnson $10,000 to carry and deliver their genetic baby. On September 19, 1990, Ms. Johnson gave birth to a 6-pound, 10-ounce (approx 3-kilogram) boy.

Anna Johnson then changed her mind and sued for custody, child support, and damages. She claimed that the couple failed to give her agreed-upon financial and emotional support. The court allowed the Calverts to have custody of the child while hearings were held to decide whether the child should be permanently placed with them or with the surrogate mother. The Calverts' lawyer suggested that Johnson never planned to turn the boy over to his genetic parents because she wanted a white child. In her own defense, Johnson testified that she had grown attached to the baby as it developed in her womb. Finally, the judge ruled that the Calverts "are the only parents of the baby boy delivered from Anna Johnson's body on September 19." He firmly rejected the possibility of three parents on the grounds that it would be confusing to the child.[2]

Dr. Michelle Harrison, a psychiatrist and family physician, served as an expert witness for Anna Johnson. She eloquently presented an argument for Anna Johnson playing a role in the boy's life. According to Ms. Harrison, "When a couple decides to implant their embryo in the body of another woman, whether she is a paid or volunteer surrogate, that woman becomes a part of the child's life.

114

While the genetic parents may perceive the woman simply as a vehicle or a house, it is unlikely that these will be comforting images for the child. The child who has never met his father is not comforted by the thought that 'it was just some DNA in a dish' or 'it was just some DNA on a one-night fling.' "

Dr. Harrison went on to assert that the Calverts cannot pretend that their child's life began at birth. That was when their life with him began, says Dr. Harrison. But the baby's life actually began nine months earlier, when as an embryo he was implanted in the surrogate mother's womb. Dr. Harrison believes that by denying the child the mother who carried him, the Calverts are depriving him of his human birthright. "The Calverts are this child's link to his genetic past. Anna Johnson is his link to his human past."[3]

Dr. Harrison acknowledges that the Calverts can choose to conceal the child's origins from him and pretend that Mrs. Calvert gave birth to him. However, she believes that here, too, as in any adoption, family secrets can destroy the very foundation of security and trust that every family needs.

▲ SURROGACY CENTERS CLAIM SUCCESS

Although cases such as the above reveal the problems with surrogacy, there are many other cases that never make headlines because they are apparently successful for all involved. Dr. Betty Aigen, the founder and director of the Surrogate Mother Program in New York City, is herself the mother of a child delivered by a surrogate after Dr. Aigen had three miscarriages and chose surrogacy as her final hope for having a family. She interviewed some 100 people; among them, Ms. Whitehead, before settling on her choice of surrogate. The woman she chose was a thirty-two-year-old grade school principal with a husband and three children. Aigen and the woman met each other and built a relationship of empathy and trust. It was a good experience for both of them, the kind that creates a new happy family, but doesn't make the six o'clock news.

According to Aigen, "Proper screening would have disqualified someone as ambivalent as Mary Beth."[4] Karen Chaves, of the Center for Surrogate Parenting in California, would agree. She claims that there have been approximately 5,000 surrogate births and of these, only fourteen have not worked well (the surrogate changes her mind or the child is taken from the couple). That is less than half of one percent. The Center claims that it has been matching couples and surrogate mothers for the last twelve years, and in more than 200 births has never had a surrogate refuse to give up her child. Ms. Chaves credits their record to their careful screening and counseling programs.

"We take four months to screen the surrogate and her husband before they even come near any couples,"she explains. The Center makes sure that the surrogate and her husband are positive that this is the right thing for them. The Center has certain guidelines for a surrogate mother: her family must be established and include at least one child of her own, she and her husband must want no more children, she must be between the ages of twenty-one and thirty-six, and she must not be receiving any kind of welfare payment.

The age requirement is set so that the woman is mature enough to make the decision to be a surrogate. The Center wants only surrogates who have had a child so that their fertility has already been proved. They don't want surrogates to work with a couple for a whole year, with a lot of heartbreak involved, only to find that they themselves cannot have children. "That's a hard way to find out, and it's very hard for the couple as well," says Ms. Chaves. Another reason the Center wants surrogates who have given birth is that "if a woman never had her own child, she does not know what it's like to give up that child." And, although the surrogates are paid a fee, the Center does not want money to be the motivating factor in a woman's decision to be a surrogate. They require that either the surrogate or her husband be working.

They find that the surrogates, in the majority of cases, are women who have had an abortion in the past or have known someone who cannot have biological children. "If you have a sister or a friend who's experiencing infertility, you really feel for these people when they come around and see your children and then you decide you want to do something about this,"says Ms. Chaves. Dr. Aigen noted that most prevalent among her surrogate applicants is a love of being pregnant. Other reasons include having been adopted or having known someone who was adopted.

The Center for Surrogate Parenting requires that couples and surrogates be screened thoroughly. Couples must have a letter from a qualified doctor documenting their medical problem. The Center will not work with couples who simply do not want to carry their own child. They require a medical basis—if not infertility, it might be a hysterectomy, or a heart problem that prevents a woman from carrying a child herself. They also require that the couple and the surrogate meet with a counselor to determine if they are psychologically sound enough to handle this very emotional experience. "Remember,"says Ms. Chaves, "surrogacy may not work. You may make six attempts and still have no child. There's no guarantee that it will happen on the first attempt. You have to be ready to deal with all the ups and downs that go along with surrogacy."

Occasionally, the Center will reject couples on a psychological basis. For instance, they had a couple request a surrogate a month after their seventeen-year-old son died in an accident. The Center rejected them because it was felt that they were not yet ready for a second child, but were just trying to replace their first child. The Center advised them to seek counseling and come to terms with the fact that they no longer had their first son. Thus, if they wanted a child, it was because they wanted a second child, not a replacement for the first. "That's not fair to the surrogate,"said Ms. Chaves.

The Center provides a staff attorney for the couple, and pays for the surrogate to choose an independent lawyer so that she is in no way influenced by anyone at the Center."We want to make sure that she and her husband really want to do this. Generally an attorney out there will say 'don't do this,' and you get a very balanced person."

The Center supports open adoption: the couple is expected to meet the surrogate, her husband, and her children. Everyone involved decides if they want to work together. Later on, they are expected to stay in contact. Some surrogates from the Center may exchange no more than one letter a year; others go to the other extreme and become part of the family, spending holidays together. Those who do not want an open arrangement cannot enter their program, says Ms. Chaves.

The cost for this road to parenting is not inexpensive. In fact, to obtain a genetic link to a child can run anywhere from approximately $22,000 to $42,000. There is an additional fee if the first attempt at surrogacy is unsuccessful.

Although there have been several cases of family surrogacy in which one sister carries a child for another sister, Ms. Chaves is wary of such situations. "When your sister comes to you and says 'I can't have a baby , will you carry one for me?' there is a pressure to say yes," she says, and that can create many problems. The Center relies on counseling to bring these problems to the surface. The psychologist may ask the potential surrogate to imagine what she would do if her sister's husband started abusing the child. Would she demand the child back? What if her sister got divorced? Would she want the child back then? Or, what if she didn't like the way her sister was bringing up the child?

According to Ms. Chaves, when surrogacy works, "it really works well." Dr. Aigen, whose husband and she built their program out of their own search for a surrogate, thinks that surrogates are wonderful and special. "It feels so good helping couples like myself have a family,"she says. Although her program supports open adoption, the program allows for confidential as well as open surrogacies, always respecting the wishes of the individuals involved. She has worked with people who all wished anonymity, as well as those like the surrogate who was a college student planning to go on to law school who spent the last months of her pregnancy living in the potential adoptive parents' home.

Dr. Aigen is critical of programs that ignore the surrogate after delivery. She has found that surrogates "tend to have a strong sense of ethics and morality and are responsible, rational human beings." What most people don't realize is how important and what a powerful experience it is for these surrogate mothers,"she said."It permits them to provide something of value to infertile couples." Dr. Aigen says that quite often surrogates have college degrees, and sometimes they are better educated and wealthier than the couple who has chosen them. In her experience, the majority of infertile couples seeking a surrogate are middle-class and not very well off financially. As for the children themselves, they are being raised in "the most stable and loving homes our country can provide." She notes that "Only four of the couples who are parents of children born to surrogate mothers have divorced. This is less than 1 percent in contrast to our national divorce rate of 49 percent."

To those who want to enact antisurrogacy bills, she further asserts that the proposed legislation "infringes on your Constitutional Right to Privacy and Right to Procreate . . . to deny this option to infertile couples and surrogates is narrow, sexist, and arbitrary."

While surrogacy parenting has many supporters, organizations like the National Coalition Against Surrogacy continue to try to get antisurrogacy bills passed. These would make commercialized childbearing contracts illegal. The Coalition believes that surrogacy contracts exploit women emotionally, physically, and economically. Its fact sheet notes that surrogates are "routinely forced to undergo hormone injections, amniocentesis, diet controls, and an array of genetic probes and tests at the discretion of the client. Agreements often stipulate that the mother agree to abort the fetus on demand if and when the client desires to terminate the 'service.' Women sign away their parental rights before their pregnancy, when they are unable to predict their future feelings about their child."[5]

Opponents to surrogacy further claim that most "baby brokers" routinely appeal to economically disenfranchised women in desperate need of the $10,000 fee. In addition to citing headline cases in which surrogates fought to keep the child they carried, opponents argue that surrogacy cheapens life to the status of a commercial product, and constitutes a form of exploitation of a woman's body.

In its position paper, the American Medical Association's Council on Ethical and Judicial Affairs reported that in its opinion, "Surrogate motherhood does not represent a satisfactory reproductive alternative for people who wish to become parents because of the many associated ethical, legal, psychological, societal, and financial concerns." The Council voiced its concern that in surrogacy parenting, unlike adoption, the prospective parents are often not investigated. Furthermore, they noted that in the birth of a defective child through surrogacy, the situation may arise in which neither the surrogate nor the prospective adoptive parents may want or be able to assume the responsibilities of parenthood.

Finally, what do you tell the children? Those who oppose surrogacy say that adoptive parents can tell their children that their mother loved them so much that she gave them up because that was what was best for them. But what do the parents of a surrogate baby say, ask the critics. They suggest that children can suffer psychological consequences if they think that their mother gave birth simply because she needed $10,000.[6] Meanwhile, the Center for Surrogate Parenting reports that couples who have created their families by surrogacy are counseled about how to tell their children the truth about their birth. The Center's philosophy is that children should not be lied to. Its counselors help couples decide how to tell children the truth, so that they do not find out at a later stage and suffer because the parents have kept the truth from them. "It just all depends on how you present it to them,"says Ms. Chaves."The couple and the surrogate are always going to give us their telephone numbers and addresses. If the child ever wants to contact the surrogate, with the parents' permission, they certainly can. We make sure we always have updates of information."

▲ OTHER THIRD-PARTY REPRODUCTION TECHNIQUES

While heated controversy over surrogate parenting continues to grow, so does the number of third-party reproduction techniques available. Today, more and more infertile women are being implanted with embryos conceived in a laboratory from their husband's sperm and an egg from another woman. As one doctor put it, this is like "adopting an embryo instead of a baby." This fairly recent procedure was first performed in Australia in 1984. Currently, there are fewer than 500 "donor babies" in the United States, with nearly fifty American hospitals using the procedure. It costs about $9,000 per attempt, and the rate of success varies from 30 to 40 percent.

The average egg donor is believed to act out of altruism

since the procedure is time-consuming, uncomfortable, and carries a slight risk of leaving her infertile. She receives an injection of drugs every day to induce her ovaries to produce more than one egg at a time. For three weeks, she has her blood checked and her eggs' maturity monitored daily. When the eggs are ripe, they are surgically removed from her ovary, and then fertilized with sperm from the recipient's husband. After fertilization, the embryo is transferred to the recipient's uterus. The donor's role is over, yet she is always genetically linked to the child. According to psychologist Linda Applegarth, who screens participants at New York Hospital-Cornell Medical Center, "This third party will always be a factor in their lives."[7]

Although many donors do not feel they are contributing any more than tissue, some lawyers warn that it is inevitable that a donor will eventually sue for parental rights. There is a legal precedent: a case in Oregon in which a man whose sperm was used for artificial insemination recently won visitation rights. Many ethical and legal questions are still in the wings, destined to surface and make headline news in the years to come.

As in surrogacy cases, doctors seek egg donors who are not likely to cause problems later on. Their prime candidate is a stable married woman under thirty-five with all the children she and her husband want. An egg donor usually receives about $1,500. The price, which often doesn't compensate for lost work time, signifies that the donors are not doing it for the money. One donor claims to do it because "I get sheer enjoyment out of it." She likes knowing the children she has helped conceive, and requests annual photographs from the parents.

It is very likely that by the next century, the scientific innovations at our disposal will make today's heated surrogacy controversies seem rather tame. Day by day, new techniques are transforming our concept of what a parent is. For instance, doctors are currently working on fetal adoption, in which a fetus is removed from the biological mother and transplanted to and carried to term by, the adoptive mother, or delivered from an incubator. The question of who is a parent will likely be as confusing as the larger question: what is a family?

ADOPTION
CONTROVERSIES
REVISITED

As you realize by now, there are many controversies about our current adoption practices. Yet one thing is clear: for hundreds of thousands of people in all walks of life, adoption is a viable and positive way to create a loving family. While people will continue to argue over the fine points of adoption, birthparents and adoptive parents will continue to be thankful for each others' existence. Their stories are often poignant and filled with emotion.

Susan S., a New York film producer, went through eight years of trying to become pregnant before she and her husband accepted their infertility and chose to adopt. She remembers the torture of waking up every morning and putting a basal thermometer in her mouth to check her temperature (to see if she was ovulating), and trying everything the doctors suggested, only to be disappointed every month. Susan, who doubts that anyone who hasn't gone through infertility can imagine what it is like, claims to have had the best baby shower in the entire world. "At it I took my basal thermometer and threw it out the window. That was one of the highlights of my life. It was over. I didn't have to deal with it anymore."

For Susan, adoption was a blessing, a way to fulfill her

desire to have the children she and her husband, Steve, were ready to love. A year after they adopted their first son, they adopted another infant boy. The birthmothers of both boys were not ready to take on the responsibility of being parents, and each of them voiced their gratitude to Susan and Steve. From Susan's viewpoint, "There is no question in my mind that it is a selfless thing for a young girl to want a better life for another human being than she can offer."

Susan's story is just one of many that seem to be turning out happily for everyone involved. And Susan's family, created after much grief, appears to be thriving. But it is hard to draw conclusions from hers or from any family created through adoption; each of them has its own story to tell. In the future, as the different kinds of adoptive families continue to grow, no doubt the individual differences between adoptive families will be even greater than today. For this reason, adoption experts emphasize the need for an individualistic approach to adoption.[1]

Birthparents, adoptive parents, and adoptees will continue to struggle with the many issues that the option of adoption brings up. At the same time, the system itself will surely keep changing, as those in the adoption community keep trying to do their best to improve this alternative way to make a family. Foster care, too, is destined to change, as experts try to make it work better for those it is meant to serve, and try to encourage people who are set on adopting infants to consider giving permanent homes to children in foster care instead.

▲ WISH LISTS FOR TOMORROW

Many people in the adoption community have wish lists, since the system is still far from perfect. Clinical social worker Priscilla Misner says that one of her wishes is for foster care to be able to help families in trouble understand what needs to happen in order for children who have been removed to come back. The system must then be able to provide the help needed. Her concern comes from her awareness of how devastating it is to children "to know that the people taking care of them are not in charge, there is a system out there that can remove them at any minute." She would like to see the development of good family preservation services, but if families are offered help and do not accept it, Misner believes that other plans have to be made for the children.

Her wish list also includes more openness, which she sees as today's main issue in adoption. She would like the secrecy eliminated for adoptees as well as for searchers. However, she doesn't think that openness can be effective unless adoption is demystified. "People who give up their children should see it as a choice they're making; it doesn't have to be such a secret," she says.

Another person whose wish list includes an acceptance of choices is Patti Caldwell of Southern Arizona Planned Parenthood. She would like counselors and others to show their support for young pregnant women, regardless of their decision, and to let them know that society doesn't value one option over others. Caldwell doesn't believe that there is one best choice. "I think it's very individual to the person, to the social structure, and to the family," she says. "And what is their best choice today might be entirely different a year from now and that's fine."

Caldwell would also like schools to provide comprehensive sex education that includes lessons on unplanned pregnancy and pregnancy options, with full information about adoptions and adoption processes, abortion, and pregnancy.

Glen Hester's wish also involves changes in education. He would like schools to do a better job of teaching children how to "make families." "We create social illiterates," he says, "We do not empower children to have authority over their own lives." He would also like more children to understand that just because their family failed doesn't mean that they failed.

Among therapist Joe Soll's many wishes is a way for pregnant women to receive counseling as quickly as possible so that those who want to keep their children can find a way to do so. Another of his wishes is to change laws as well as to change sentiments. He hopes for a future in which we will be able to develop a uniform adoption law for every state; this would be produced by an eleven-member national committee of commissioners and adoption experts.

In the meantime, while the fires of adoption controversies continue to rage, the voices of adoption seem to be echoing each other in several ways. Many agree that adoption is a special way to create a family, and that those involved in or touched by adoptive situations need to become more sensitive to each others' feelings and needs. Birthparents, adoptive parents, and adoptees all need to consider each other. Those who work with members of the triad also need to respect those in it. And the general public needs to be more informed and supportive of those faced with the hard choices that adoption and foster care require.

There are no easy resolutions to the many issues that adoption and foster care raise in our society. Many of these issues are related to each other, and many have been created as the children available for adoption change. No doubt the future holds situations and controversies we cannot yet imagine, and new studies will probably shift our thinking again and again. To William Pierce of the National Committee for Adoption some of the new adoption practices are equivalent to the use of a drug whose explosive side effects won't be known for twenty years.[2] Yet, on the brighter side, there are the stories of people like Susan, stories we hear day after day about loving families made possible through adoption.

If we can remember that the children are the focus, although every member of the triad is important, we can begin to look beyond the controversies to the ultimate goal: using all the means available within today's society to create the healthiest families possible.

ORGANIZATIONS AND SOURCES OF ADDITIONAL INFORMATION

▲ GENERAL INFORMATION ABOUT ADOPTION

National Adoption Information Clearinghouse
Suite 600, 1400 Eye St. NW
Washington, DC 20005
202-842-1919

National Committee for Adoption
1930 17th St. NW
Washington DC 20009
202-328-1200

▲ INFORMATION FOR SPECIAL INTEREST GROUPS

BIRTHFATHERS

National Organization for Birthfathers and Adoption
Reform
P.O. Box 50
Punta Gorda, FL 33951
813-575-0948

BIRTHPARENTS

Concerned United Birthparents
2000 Walker Street
Des Moines, IA 50317
800-822-2777

INFERTILITY COUNSELING

Resolve
1310 Broadway
Somerville, MA 02144
617-623-0744

FOREIGN ADOPTION

Holt International Children's Services
P.O. Box 2880
Eugene, OR 97402-9970
503-687-2202

Adoption Advocates International
658 Black Diamond Road
Port Angeles, WA 98362
206-452-4777

FOSTER CHILDREN

National Association of Former Foster Children Inc.
(NAFFC)
P.O. Box 060410
New Dorp Station
Staten Island, NY 10306
718-727-3250

SINGLE ADOPTIVE PARENTS

Committee for Single Adoptive Parents
P.O. Box 15084

Chevy Chase, MD 20825
202-966-6367

SEARCH GROUPS

Adoptee-Birthparent Support Network
P.O. Box 23674
L'Enfant Plaza Station
Washington, DC 20026-0674
301-464-5755,
Nonprofit search and support group for both adoptees and birthparents.

American Adoption Congress
P.O. Box 20137
Cherokee Station
New York, NY 10028-0051
Search Hotline 505-296-2198
Umbrella group for search, support, and education across the country.

International Soundex Reunion Registry
P.O. Box 2312
Carson City, NV 89702-2312
702-882-7755
Matching registry that does not perform or assist in searches. The registry is free and available to anyone 18 or older. (Write to request a registration form, enclosing a stamped, self-addressed envelope.)

Adoptees in Search
P.O. Box 41016
Bethesda, MD 20814
301-656-8555
National nonprofit adoptee advocacy organization. Searches on behalf of adoptees and has its own registry.

Adoptees Liberty Movement Association
P.O. Box 154
Washington Bridge Station
New York, NY 10033
212-581-1568
Has its own registry.

SPECIAL NEEDS ADOPTION

National Resource Center for Special Needs Adoption
16250 Northland Drive, Suite 120
Southfield, MI 48075
313-443-7080

National Adoption Center
1218 Chestnut Street
Philadelphia, PA 19107
215-925-0200

SURROGACY

The Surrogate Mother Program
Dr. Betsy P. Aigen
220 West 93rd Street, Suite 1A
New York, NY 10025
(212) 496-1070
Provides general information, research, consultation, and referral on surrogate parenting to surrogates and to couples.

American Organization of Surrogate Parenting
Practioners
Dr. Betsy P. Aigen
220 West 93rd Street, Suite 1A
New York, NY 10025
(212) 496-1070
Organization of surrogate agencies to protect children born through surrogacy.

The Foundation on Economic Trends
1130 17th Street, NW, Suite 630
Washington, DC 20036
(202) 466-2823
Provides anti-surrogacy information.

SOURCE NOTES

CHAPTER 1:
THE HUMAN SIDE OF ADOPTION

1. "Unwed mothers: 1 in 4 in '80," *Tucson Citizen*, Dec. 13, 1991.
2. Joan Beck, "Real-world ills demand moral messages," *Tucson Citizen*, Sept. 26, 1991.
3. Barbara Kantrowitz, "Homeroom," *Newsweek Special Issue*, Summer/Fall 1990, p. 50–52

CHAPTER 2:
TODAY'S OPTIONS FOR UNWED PREGNANT TEENAGERS

1. T.R. Reid, "Abortion and the Adoption Option," *Washington Post*, Aug. 15, 1989, Health section.
2. Gina Kolata, "Ruling Inspires Groups to Fight Harder," *New York Times*, June 30, 1992.
3. Kantrowitz, "Homeroom," p. 52.
4. Ibid.
5. T.R. Reid, "Abortion and the Adoption Option."

6. Hal Aigner, *Adoption In America Coming Of Age.* (Greenbriar, Calif: Paradigm Press, rev., 1992), p. 34.
7. Personal correspondence with Kathy Harris, co-author of *Transracial Adoption*.

CHAPTER 3:
OPEN VERSUS CLOSED ADOPTIONS

1. Cynthia Crossen, "In Today's Adoptions, the Biological Parents Are Calling the Shots," *The Wall Street Journal*, Sept. 14, 1989.
2. James Lardner, "Open Adoption and Closed Minds," *Washington Post*, Dec. 31, 1989.
3. Lincoln Caplan, *Open Adoption*. (New York: Farrar, Straus & Giroux, 1990), p. 92.
4. Ruth G. McRoy et al., "Adoption Revelation and Communication Issues: Implications for Practice." *Families in Society: The Journal of Contemporary Human Services.* May/June 1989. p. 31.
5. Crossen, "In Today's Adoptions."

CHAPTER 4:
AGENCY VERSUS INDEPENDENT ADOPTIONS

1. Lois Gilman, *The Adoption Resource Book*. (New York: Harper Perennial, Rev. 1992), p. 73.
2. Laura Mansnerus, "Private Adoptions Aided By Expanding Network," *The New York Times*, Oct. 5, 1989.
3. Bonnie D. Gradstein, Marc Gradstein, and Robert H. Glass, "Private Adoption," *Fertility and Sterility.* Apr. 1982, pp. 458–51.
4. Edmund Blair Bolles, *A Guide To Creating Your New Family: The Penguin Adoption Handbook*. (New York: Viking Press, 1984), p. 134.
5. Mansnerus, "Private Adoptions Aided. . . ."

CHAPTER 5:
TRANSRACIAL ADOPTIONS

1. Constance Pohl and Kathy Harris, *Transracial Adoption: Children and Parents Speak*. (New York: Franklin Watts, 1992).
2. Helene Lorber, "Interracial Adoption: Child's Ethnicity, Culture Usually Swallowed by New Family's Traditions." *Arizona Daily Star*. Oct. 9, 1990.
3. Pohl and Harris, p. 29.
4. "Nobody's Children," *Time*, Oct. 9, 1989, p. 95.
5. Lorber, "Interracial Adoption."
6. Lois Gilman, *The Adoption Resource Book*. (New York: Harper Perennial, rev.1992), pp. 26–29.
7. Rita Simon and Howard Altstein, *Transracial Adoptees and Their Families*. (New York: Praeger, 1987).
8. Simon and Altstein.
9. Beth Brophy, "The unhappy politics of interracial adoption," *U.S. News and World Report*, Nov. 13, 1989, pp. 73–74.
10. Brophy, p. 74.
11. Miriam Davidson, "Trail of Tears," *Tucson Weekly*, Nov. 23, 1989.
12. Davidson, "Trail of Tears."
13. Bart Eisenberg, "Road to Foreign Adoption Gets Rockier," *The Christian Science Monitor*, February 28, 1990.
14. Kathleen Hunt, "The Romanian Baby Bazaar," *The New York Times Magazine*, March 24, 1991, p. 24.
15. Lisa O'Rourke and Ruth Hubbell, with Sherrell Goolsby, "Intercountry Adoption," (Washington: *National Adoption Information Clearinghouse* Rev. 1991), p. 10.
16. Eisenberg, "Road to Foreign Adoption. . . ."
17. Karen Howze, "Mixing Cultures," *USA WEEKEND*, Nov. 2–4 , 1990.

CHAPTER 6:
FOSTER CARE

1. Barbara Kantrowitz, with John McCormick and Pat Wingery, "Children Lost in the Quagmire," *Newsweek*, May 13, 1991.
2. Patrick O'Brien, "Youth Homelessness and the Lack of Adoption Planning For Older Foster Children: Are They Related?" (position paper)

CHAPTER 7:
SPECIAL-NEEDS ADOPTIONS AND UNCONVENTIONAL PARENTS

1. "Countering the Call for a Return to Orphanages." *The Roundtable: Journal of the National Resource Center for Special Needs Adoption*, Number 1, 1991. p 11.
2. Barbara Maddux, "Mother Love," *Life*, May, 1992, pp. 49–56.
3. Glenna Wooderson, "Single Parents Making Progress," (Washington: National Adoption Information Center).
4. Joan F. Shireman and Penny R. Johnson, "Single Parent Adoptions: A Longitudinal Study," *Children and Youth Services Review*, 1985, p. 332.

CHAPTER 8:
RIGHTS OF BIRTHFATHERS

1. Paul Sachdev, "The Birth Father: A Neglected Element in the Adoption Equation," *Families in Society: The Journal of Contemporary Human Services*," March, 1991, pp. 131–139.
2. Eva Y. Deykin et al., "Fathers of Adopted Children: A Study of the Impact of Child Surrender on Birthfathers,"

American Orthopsychiatric Association, Inc., Apr. 1988, pp. 240–248.
3. Hal Aigner, *Adoption In America Coming of Age*, (Greenbriar, Calif.: Paradigm Press, rev. 1992), p. 70.
4. Elizabeth Kolbert, "Fathers' Rights on Adoption Are Expanded," *New York Times*, July 11, 1990.

CHAPTER 9:
SEARCHES

1. David M. Brodzinsky, Marshall D. Schechter, and Robin Marantz Henig, *Being Adopted: The Lifelong Search for Self*. (New York: Doubleday, 1992), p. 144.
2. Laura Watkins Lewis, "In Search of Daniel," *Washington Post*, Feb. 13, 1990, Health section.
3. Mary McGrory, "Adoption's Lasting Anguish," *Washington Post*, Aug. 8, 1990.
4. Lewis "In Search of Daniel."
5. *New York Times*, Nov. 11, 1990, New Jersey section.
6. Elizabeth Taylor, "Are You My Mother?", *Time*, Oct. 9, 1989, p. 90.

CHAPTER 10:
ARE ADOPTEES DIFFERENT?

1. Lawrence Caplan, *Open Adoption* (New York: Farrar, Straus & Giroux, 1990), p. 80.
2. David M. Brodzinsky, Marshall D. Schechter, and Robin Marantz Henig, *Being Adopted: The Lifelong Search for Self* (New York: Doubleday, 1992), p. 11.
3. Ibid. p. 110.
4. Ibid. p. 102.
5. Caplan, p. 34.
6. Brodzinsky, Schechter, and Henig, p. 186.

CHAPTER 11:
SURROGATE MOTHERING

1. Linda Arking, "Searching for a very SPECIAL WOMAN," *McCalls*, June 1987, p. 55–56.
2. "Surrogate accused of wanting white child," *Tucson Citizen*, October 11, 1990.
3. Michelle Harrison, "The Baby With Two Mothers," *The Wall Street Journal*, October 23, 1990, p. 31.
4. Arking, "Searching."
5. Surrogacy Fact Sheet (Washington: The Foundation on Economic Trends).
6. Katha Politt, "The Strange Case of Baby M." *The Nation*, May 23, 1987, p. 66.
7. Anna Quindlen, "Life in the 30's," *The New York Times*, Feb. 10, 1988.

CHAPTER 12:
ADOPTION CONTROVERSIES REVISITED

1. David Brodzinsky, Marshall D. Schechter, and Robin Marantz Henig, *Being Adopted: The Lifelong Search for Self* (New York: Doubleday, 1992), p. 190.
2. Cynthia Crossen, "In Today's Adoptions, the Biological Parents Are Calling the Shots," *The Wall Street Journal*, Sept. 14, 1989.

GLOSSARY

ADOPTED CHILD SYNDROME—Concept based on belief that adoptees have more psychological and emotional problems than other children

ADOPTEE—Person whose birthparent (or birthparents) gives up legal rights so that he or she can legally become the son or daughter of adoptive parents

ADOPTION—Legal process by which parental rights are transferred from a child's birthparent(s) to his or her adoptive parent(s)

ADOPTIVE PARENT—Adult who is granted legal rights and responsibilities for a child who was born to someone else.

AGENCY ADOPTION—Adoption coordinated by a licensed state or private adoption agency

ARTIFICIAL INSEMINATION—Process by which a man's sperm is introduced, without sexual contact, into the female reproductive organs of a surrogate mother. The surrogate then carries the baby to term, after which it is adopted by the man's spouse; it is already legally the man's child since it was conceived with his sperm.

ATTACHMENT—Process by which baby and parent bond

to each other after baby is born. May refer to mother or father.

BIOLOGICAL PARENT—Birthparent of child; parent to whom child was born

BIRTHPARENT—Biological parent of child; person whose genes the child has

BONDING—Process that takes place between parent and baby. Some use term to explain process that takes place when baby is in mother's womb. Others interchange the word with "attachment."

CLOSED ADOPTION—Adoption in which birthparent(s) and adoptive parent(s) have no contact or ongoing communication, and few facts about them are exchanged

CROSS-CULTURAL ADOPTION—Placing a child of one culture with a family of another culture

EGG DONOR—Woman whose egg is combined with the sperm of a man in a laboratory, and then replanted in the body of the man's infertile spouse or partner

FETAL ADOPTION—Procedure of the future in which fetus is removed from a biological mother and is either transplanted into the body of an adoptive mother, who carries it to term, or is delivered from an incubator

FINALIZATION—Court procedure that makes an adoption binding and irrevocable

FOSTER CARE—Temporary placement of a child in the care of a foster parent or parents without legally transferring to them the rights to the child

GENETIC LINK—Inheritance of genetic material from birthparent to birthchild

GENETIC MATERIAL—The heredity material of cells that are passed on from birthparents to child and control many characteristics of that child

HOME STUDY—Screening of potential adoptive parents to determine if they will make good parents. Home studies may include visits to the adoptive parents' home, interviews, and group counseling sessions.

IDENTIFIED ADOPTION—Adoption in which birthparent(s) and adoptive parent(s) establish contact outside of an agency, but use an agency's services to finalize their adoption agreement

INDEPENDENT (PRIVATE) ADOPTION—Adoption arranged outside of an adoption agency, most usually by a doctor or lawyer. Such adoptions are not legal in all states.

INFERTILITY—Inability to become pregnant and have children

KINSHIP PROGRAM—Adoption strategy that involves contacting relatives of children who are ready for adoption or being raised in foster homes and encouraging the relatives to adopt the child

LEGAL RISK FOSTER PARENT—Foster parent who cares for a child, intending to adopt the child when he or she is legally free to be adopted

MULTIPLE PLACEMENTS—Situation in which a child is sent to many foster homes

NONIDENTIFYING INFORMATION—General facts about birthparents, but not including their names and addresses

OPEN ADOPTION—Adoption in which the birth and adoptive families have some degree of contact and/or ongoing communication

PRIVATE ADOPTION—See Independent adoption.

RELINQUISHMENT—The signing of documents by a birthparent terminating his or her parental rights and responsibilities for a child (also known as surrender)

SEALED RECORDS—Documents and files about an adoption that are restricted by law or policy from being seen by the public

SEARCH REGISTRY—State or private system through which separated family members may register to be matched and reunited

SINGLE ADOPTIVE PARENT—An unmarried man or woman who adopts a child

SPECIAL-NEEDS CHILD—Child who is considered harder to adopt than a healthy white infant. Special-needs

143

children include infants who are nonwhite, older children, sibling groups, and children who are physically and/or emotionally challenged.

SURROGACY (GESTATIONAL)—Process by which the sperm and egg of a couple are united in a laboratory, then implanted in the body of a surrogate mother, who carries the baby to term

SURROGATE MOTHER—Woman who acts as a third party in a pregnancy, and carries a baby to term for a couple who in some way are infertile

THERAPEUTIC FOSTER PARENTS—Specially trained or experienced adults who care for foster children with multiple problems, often of an emotional nature

TRANSRACIAL ADOPTION—Adoption of a child of a race that is different from that of the adopting family

TRIAD—The three categories of people directly involved in an adoption: 1) the adoptee, 2) the birthparent(s), and 3) the adoptive parent(s)

BIBLIOGRAPHY

BOOKS

Aigner, Hal. *Adoption In America Coming Of Age*. rev. ed. Greenbriar, Calif.: Paradigm Press, 1992.

Arms, Suzanne. *To Love and Let Go*. New York: Alfred A. Knopf, 1983.

Askin, Jane, and Oskam, Bob. *Search: A Handbook for Adoptees and Birthparents*. 2nd ed. New York: Harper and Row, 1992.

Bolles, Edmund Blair. *The Penguin Adoption Handbook*. New York: Viking Press, 1984.

Brodzinsky, David M., Schechter, Marshall D., and Henig, Robin Marantz. *Being Adopted: The Lifelong Search for Self*. New York: Doubleday, 1992.

Caplan, Lincoln. *Open Adoption*. New York: Farrar, Straus & Giroux, 1990

Gilman, Lois. *The Adoption Resource Book*. rev. ed. New York, Harper Perennial, 1992.

Gritter, James L. *Adoption Without Fear*. San Antonio, Tex.: Corona Publishing Company, 1989.

Gudiman, Judith, and Brown, Linda. *Birth Bond*. Far Hills, N. J.: New Horizon Press, 1989.

Klunder, Virgil L. *Lifeline: The Action Guide to Adoption Search*. Cape Coral, Fla.: Caradium Publishing, 1991.

Krementz, Jill. *How It Feels To Be Adopted*. New York: Alfred A. Knopf, 1988.

Landau, Elaine. *Surrogate Mothers*. New York: Franklin Watts, 1988.

Lindsay, Jeanne Warren. *Pregnant Too Soon: Adoption Is An Option*. rev. ed. Buena Park, Calif.: Morning Glory Press, 1988.

Livingston, Carole. *Why Was I Adopted?* Secaucus, N.J.: Lyle Stuart, 1978.

McRoy, Ruth G., and Zurcher, Louis A. *Transracial and Inracial Adoptees: The Adolescent Years*. Springfield, Ill.: Charles C. Thomas, 1983.

Pohl, Constance, and Harris, Kathy. *Transracial Adoption: Children and Parents Speak*. New York: Franklin Watts, 1992.

Powledge, Fred. *The New Adoption Maze and How To Get Through It*. St. Louis, Mo.: C.V. Mosby Company, 1985.

Register, Cheri. *Are Those Kids Yours?: American Families with Children Adopted from Other Countries*. New York: Free Press, 1991.

Shapiro, Jerrold. *When Men Are Pregnant: Needs and Concerns of Expectant Fathers*. San Luis Obisbo, Calif.: Impact Pubs Cal, 1987.

Silber, Kathleen, and Speedlin, Phylis. *Dear Birthmother: Thank You for Our Baby*. San Antonio, Tex.: Corona Publishing Company, 1983.

Silber, Kathleen, and Martinez, Patricia. *Children of Open Adoption*. San Antonio, Tex.: Corona Publishing Company, 1990.

Simon, Rita J., and Altstein, Howard, eds. *Intercountry Adoption: A Multinational Perspective*. New York: Praeger, 1991.

Simon, Rita J., and Altstein, Howard. *Transracial Adoptees and Their Families*. New York: Praeger, 1987.

Witt, Reni L., and Michael, Jeannine Masterson. *Mom, I'm Pregnant! A Personal Guide for Teenagers.* New York: Stein & Day, 1982.

ARTICLES AND PAPERS

Arking, Linda. "Searching for a very SPECIAL WOMAN," *McCalls*, June 1987, p. 55–56.

Associated Press. "Court OKs limits on abortion." *Tucson Citizen*, June 29, 1992.

Associated Press. "Critics knock state's ability to regulate adoption agencies." *Tucson Citizen*, May 4, 1992.

Beck, Joan. "Real-world ills demand moral messages." *Tucson Citizen*, Sept. 26, 1991.

Blumenthal, Ralph. "At issue: who best to care for a child, body and soul." *The New York Times*, July 22, 1991.

Bronson, Peter. "An alternative to abortion: unplanned parenthood." *Tucson Citizen*, October 3, 1991.

Brophy, Beth. "The unhappy politics of interracial adoption." *U.S. News and World Report*, Nov. 13, 1989.

Cannella, David. "Price of adoption." *Arizona Daily Star*, Sept. 30, 1990.

Challenges, A Newsletter of the National Association of Former Foster Children, Inc.

Citizen Wire Services. "Unwed mothers: 1 in 4 in '89" *Tucson Citizen*, Dec. 13, 1991.

Clements, Mark. "Should Abortion Remain Legal?" *Parade*, May 17, 1992, p. 4–5.

"Countering the Call for a Return to Orphanages." *The Roundtable: Journal of the National Resource Center for Special Needs Adoption*, Number 1, 1991. p 11.

Crossen, Cynthia. "In Today's Adoptions, the Biological Parents Are Calling the Shots," *The Wall Street Journal*, Sept. 14, 1989.

Davidson, Miriam. "Trail of Tears." *Tucson Weekly*, Nov. 23, 1989.

Deykin, Eva Y., Patti, Patricia, and Ryan, Jon. "Fathers of Adopted Children: A study of the Impact of Child Surrender on Birthfathers." *American Orthopsychiatric Association, Inc.*, April 1988, pp. 240–248.

Dockser, Amy. "More Unwed Fathers Push For Equal Say in Adoptions." *Wall Street Journal*, Feb. 23, 1989.

Dusky, Lorraine. "The Daughter I Gave Away." *Newsweek*, March 30, 1992, pp. 12–13.

Eisenberg, Bart. "Road to Foreign Adoptions Gets Rockier." *The Christian Science Monitor.* Feb. 28, 1990.

Gibbs, Nancy. "The Baby Chase." *Time*, Oct. 9, 1989, pp. 86–89.

Glaser, Gabrielle. "Booming Polish market: blond, blue-eyed babies." *The New York Times*, April 19, 1992.

Gradstein, Bonnie D., Gradstein, Marc, and Glass, Robert H. "Private Adoption." *Fertility and Sterility.* April 1982, pp. 458–51.

Greenhouse, Steven. "French Supreme Court Rules Surrogate-Mother Agreements Illegal." *The New York Times*, June 2, 1991, p. 12N.

Harrison, Michelle. "The Baby with Two Mothers," *The Wall Street Journal*, Oct. 23, 1990, p. 31.

Henig, Robin Marantz. "Chosen and Given." *The New York Times Magazine*, September 11, 1988, pp. 70–72.

Hilts, Philip. "New Study Challenges Estimates on Odds of Adopting a Child." *The New York Times*, Dec. 10, 1990, p. B10.

Hoffman-Riem, Christa. "Disclosing Adoption." *Society*, May/June 1989, pp. 26–29.

Howze, Karen. "Mixing cultures." *USA WEEKEND*, November 2–4, 1990, p. 16.

Hunt, Kathleen. "The Romanian baby bazaar." *The New York Times Magazine*, March 24, 1991, p. 24.

Kantrowitz, Barbara. "Homeroom." *Newsweek Special Issue*, Summer/Fall 1990, p. 50–52.

Kantrowitz, Barbara, with McCormick, John, and

Wingery, Pat. "Children Lost in the Quagmire." *Newsweek*, May 13, 1991, pp. 50–52.

Kolata, Gina. "Ruling Inspires Groups to Fight Harder." *The New York Times*, June 30, 1992, p. A9.

Kolbert, Elizabeth. "Fathers Rights on Adoption Are Expanded." *New York Times*, July 11, 1990, p. B1.

Lacayo, Richard. "Nobody's Children." *Time*, Oct. 9, 1989, pp. 91–95.

Lardner, James. "Open Adoption and Closed Minds." *Washington Post*, Dec. 31, 1989, p. C3.

Letter To The Editor, *The New York Times*, Nov. 11, 1990, New Jersey section.

Lewis, Laura Watkins. "In Search of Daniel." *Washington Post* Feb. 13, 1990, Health section.

Locust, Carol. "Expatriated Indians are strangers in two cultures." *Tucson Citizen*, May 12, 1992, p. 11A.

Lorber, Helene. "Interracial Adoption." *The Arizona Daily Star*, Oct. 9, 1990, pp. C1/C3.

Maddux, Barbara. "Mother Love." *Life*, May 1992, pp. 49–56.

Mansnerus, Laura. "Private Adoptions Aided by Expanding Network." *The New York Times*, Oct. 5, 1989, p. 1.

McGrory, Mary. "Adoption's Lasting Anguish." *Washington Post*, Aug. 8, 1990, p. E1.

McGrory, Mary. "Children from the Heart." *The Washington Post*, Feb. 3, 1991, p. E1.

McRoy, Ruth G. "Adoptive Families." *Families in Society*, November 1990, p. 551.

McRoy, Ruth G., Grotevant, Harold D., Lopez, Susan Ayers, and Furuta, Ann. "Adoption Revelation and Communication Issues: Implications for Practice." *Families in Society: The Journal of Contemporary Human Services*, May/June 1989, pp. 550–553.

Nelser, Brent. "Better Adoption for Special-Needs Children." *The Christian Science Monitor*, Jan. 31, 1989, p. 18.

149

Networker Adoption Newsletter, available from Downey Side, JAF Box 110, New York, NY 10116.

O'Brien, Patrick, "Youth Homelessness and the lack of Adoption Planning for Older Foster Children: Are They Related?" (position paper)

Olwert, Carol J. "The other option is adoption for pregnant teens." *Tucson Citizen,* Dec. 5, 1991, p. 13A.

O'Rouke, Lisa, and Hubbell, Ruth, with Goolsby, Sherrell. "Intercountry Adoption." *National Adoption Information Clearinghouse.* Rev. 1991. p. 10.

"Out-of-wedlock Births Keep Climbing,"*Tucson Citizen,* Sept. 30, 1991, pp. E1–2.

Panzarine, S., and Elster, A.B. "Coping in a Group of Adolescent Expectant Fathers: An Exploratory Study." *Journal of Adolescent Health Care, 4.* 1983, pp. 117–120.

Pierce, William. "Taking Adoption Seriously." *Society,* July/ August 1990, pp. 21–24.

Politt, Katha. "The Strange Case of Baby M." *The Nation,* May 23, 1987. pp. 61–66.

Prowler, Mady. "Single Parent Adoption: What You Need to Know." Available from National Adoption Information Clearinghouse.

Quindlen, Anna. "Life in the 30's." *The New York Times,* Feb. 10, 1988.

Raymond, Barbara Bizantz. "The Woman Who Stole 5,000 Babies." *Good Housekeeping,* March 1991, p. 140, 180–186.

Reid, T. R. "Abortion and the Adoption Option." *Washington Post,* Aug. 15, 1989, Health section.

Sachdev, Paul. "The Birth Father: A Neglected Element in the Adoption Equation." *Families in Society: The Journal of Contemporary Human Services,"* March 1991, pp. 131–139.

Shireman, Joan F., and Johnson, Penny R. "Single Parent Adoptions: A Longitudinal Study." *Children and Youth Services Review,* 1985, p. 332.

Squires, Sally. "Unwanted Children Suffer Long-Term Difficulties." *Washington Post*, Aug. 15, 1989, Health section.

Surrogacy Fact Sheet. Washington, D.C. The Foundation on Economic Trends.

"Surrogate Accused of Wanting White Child." *Tucson Citizen*, Oct. 11, 1990, p. 25.

Szekely, Julie. "They Wish They'd Said 'No.' " *Tucson Citizen*, Oct. 10, 1991, p. B1.

Taylor, Elizabeth. "Are You My Mother?" *Time*, Oct. 9, 1989, p. 90.

Weizel, Richard. "Is Blood Thicker Than Adoption?" *USA Weekend*, March 20–22, 1992.

Wooderson, Glenna. "Single Parents Making Progress." National Adoption Information Center.

FOR FURTHER READING

Askin, Jane and Oskam, Bob. *Search: A Handbook for Adoptees and Birthparents*. 2nd ed. New York: Harper and Row, 1992.

Brodzinsky, David M., Schechter, Marshall D., and Henig, Robin Marantz. *Being Adopted: The Lifelong Search for Self*. New York: Doubleday, 1992.

Caplan, Lincoln. *Open Adoption*. New York: Farrar, Straus & Giroux, 1990.

Gilman, Lois. *The Adoption Resource Book*. rev. ed. New York, Harper Perennial, 1992.

Gudiman, Judith, and Brown, Linda. *Birth Bond*. Far Hills, N.J.: New Horizon Press, 1989.

Klunder, Virgil L. *Lifeline: The Action Guide to Adoption Search*. Cape Coral, Fla.: Caradium Publishing, 1991.

Krementz, Jill. *How It Feels To Be Adopted*. New York: Alfred A. Knopf, 1988.

Landau, Elaine. *Surrogate Mothers*. New York: Franklin Watts, 1988.

Lindsay, Jeanne Warren. *Pregnant Too Soon: Adoption Is An Option*. rev. ed. Buena Park, Calif.: Morning Glory Press, 1988.

Livingston, Carole. *Why Was I Adopted?* Secaucus, N. J.: Lyle Stuart, 1978.

Pohl, Constance, and Harris, Kathy. *Transracial Adoption: Children and Parents Speak.* New York: Franklin Watts, 1992.

Silber, Kathleen, and Speedlin, Phylis. *Dear Birthmother: Thank You for Our Baby.* San Antonio, Tex.: Corona Publishing Company, 1983.

Silber, Kathleen, and Martinez, Patricia. *Children of Open Adoption.* San Antonio, Tex.: Corona Publishing Company, 1990.

Witt, Reni L., and Michael, Jeannine Masterson. *Mom, I'm Pregnant! A Personal Guide for Teenagers.* New York: Stein & Day, 1982.

INDEX

American Organization of Surrogate Parenting, 132
Arizona Children's Home (ACH), 32–34, 41–43, 84
Artificial insemination, 121–122
Asian children, 61, 65–66

Bass, Peggy, 37–38
Bethany Christian Services, 41
Birthfathers, rights of, 82–88
Bonding and attachment problems, 107–109
Bouchard, Thomas J., 108
Brodzinsky, David, 105–106
Burch, Betsy, 64

Caldwell, Patti, 16–17, 19, 126
Calvert, Mark and Crispina, 114–115
Caplan, Lawrence, 37
Catholic Services, 41–42
Center for Surrogate Parenting, 116–119, 121
Chaves, Karen, 116–119, 121
Child abuse, 19, 70, 73
Child Welfare League of America, 47
Closed adoptions, 27, 29–39, 48

Cohen, Barbara, 92–93
Committee for Single Adoptive Parents, 130
Concerned United Birthparents (CUB), 97, 130
Council for Equal Rights in Adoption, 21
Cox, Susan, 65–67
Cunningham, Shawn, 86

Dawes, Janet, 32, 41, 60, 77, 84
Downey, Lexanne, 19, 25, 77, 110
Downey Side, 74–75

Federal Bureau of Investigation (FBI), 63, 64
Fetal adoption, 122–123
Foreign adoptions, 41, 60–67
Foster care, 19, 25, 53, 68–75, 125–126
Foundation on Economic Trends, The, 133

Gartrell, Kay, 91
Goldsmith, Brenda, 70, 73
Grandparents, 10, 12, 18
Greer, Lorie, 79
Gritter, Jim, 39
Guttmacher Institute, 11

ABOUT THE AUTHOR

KAREN LIPTAK has written numerous books for juvenile and young adult readers. She has authored many books for Franklin Watts, including the *North American Indian* series, *Saving the Wetlands and Their Wildlife*, and *Endangered Peoples*. She lives in Tucson, Arizona, with her daughter Jana.